Clement of Alexandria

Exhortation to the Heathen

Clement of Alexandria

Exhortation to the Heathen

Clement of Alexandria
Exhortation to the Heathen

Published by
Lighthouse Christian Publishing
SAN 257-4330
5531 Dufferin Drive
Savage, Minnesota, 55378
United States of America

www.lighthousechristianpublishing.com

Introductory Note on Clement of Alexandria

[a.d. 153–193–217.] The second century of illumination is drawing to a close, as the great name of this Father comes into view, and introduces us to a new stage of the Church's progress. From Britain to the Ganges it had already made its mark. In all its Oriental identity, we have found it vigorous in Gaul and penetrating to other regions of the West. From its primitive base on the Orontes, it has extended itself to the deltas of the Nile; and the Alexandria of Apollos and of St. Mark has become the earliest seat of Christian learning. There, already, have the catechetical schools gathered the finest intellectual trophies of the Cross; and under the aliment of its library springs up something like a Christian university.
Pantænus, "the Sicilian bee" from the flowery fields of Enna, comes to frame it by his industry, and store it with the sweets of his eloquence and wisdom. Clement, who had followed Tatian to the East, tracks Pantænus to Egypt, and comes with his Attic scholarship to be his pupil in the school of Christ. After Justin and Irenæus, he is to be reckoned the founder of Christian literature; and it is noteworthy how sublimely he begins to treat Paganism as a creed outworn, to be dismissed with contempt, rather than seriously wrestled with any longer.

His merciless exposure of the entire system of "lords many and gods many," seems to us, indeed, unnecessarily offensive. Why not spare us such details? But let us reflect, that, if such are our Christian instincts of delicacy, we owe it to this great reformer in no small proportion. For not content to show the Pagans that the very atmosphere was polluted by their mythologies, so that Christians, turn which way they would, must encounter pestilence, he becomes the ethical philosopher of Christians; and while he proceeds to dictate, even in minute details, the transformations to which the faithful must subject themselves in order "to escape the pollutions of the world," he sketches in outline the reformations which the Gospel imposes on society, and which nothing but the Gospel has ever enabled mankind to realize. "For with a celerity unsurpassable, and a benevolence to which we have ready access," says Clement, "the Divine Power hath filled the universe with the seed of salvation." Socrates and Plato had talked sublimely four hundred years before; but Lust and Murder were yet the gods of Greece, and men and women were like what they worshipped. Clement had been their disciple; but now, as the disciple of Christ, he was to exert a power over men and manners, of which they never dreamed.

Alexandria becomes the brain of Christendom: its heart was yet beating at Antioch, but the West was still receptive only, its hands and arms stretched forth towards the sunrise for further enlightenment. From the East it had obtained the Scriptures and their authentication, and from the same source was deriving the canons, the liturgies, and the creed of Christendom. The universal language of Christians is Greek. To a pagan emperor who had outgrown the ideas of Nero's time, it was no longer Judaism; but it was not less an Oriental superstition, essentially Greek in its features and its dress. "All the churches of the West," says the historian of Latin Christianity, "were Greek religious colonies. Their language was Greek, their organization Greek, their writers Greek, their Scriptures and their ritual were Greek. Through Greek, the communications of the churches of the West were constantly kept up with the East. . . . Thus the Church at Rome was but one of a confederation of Greek religious republics founded by Christianity." Now this confederation was the Holy Catholic Church.

Every Christian must recognize the career of Alexander, and the history of his empire, as an immediate precursor of the Gospel. The patronage of letters by the Ptolemies at Alexandria, the translation of the Hebrew Scriptures into the dialect of the Hellenes, the creation of a new terminology in the language of the Greeks, by which ideas of faith and of truth might find access to the mind of a heathen world, —these were preliminaries to the preaching of the Gospel to mankind, and to the composition of the New Testament of our Lord and Savior. He Himself had prophetically visited Egypt, and the idols were now to be removed before his presence. There a powerful Christian school was to make itself felt for ever in the definitions of orthodoxy; and in a new sense was that prophecy to be understood, "Out of Egypt have I called my Son."

The genius of Apollos was revived in his native city. A succession of doctors was there to arise, like him, "eloquent men, and mighty in the Scriptures." Clement tells us of his masters in Christ, and how, coming to Pantænus, his soul was filled with a deathless element of divine knowledge. He speaks of the apostolic tradition as received through his teachers hardly at second-hand. He met in that school, no doubt, some, at least, who recalled Ignatius and Polycarp; some, perhaps, who as children had heard St. John when he could only exhort his congregations to "love one another." He could afterwards speak of himself as in the next succession after the apostles.

He became the successor of Pantænus in the catechetical school, and had Origen for his pupil, with other eminent men. He was also ordained a presbyter. He seems to have compiled his *Stromata* in the reigns of Commodus and Severus. If, at this time, he was about forty years of age, as seems likely, we must conceive of his birth at Athens, while Antoninus Pius was emperor, while Polycarp was yet living, and while Justin and Irenæus were in their prime.

Alexander, bishop of Jerusalem, speaks of Clement, in turn, as his master: "for we acknowledge as fathers those blessed saints who are gone before us, and *to whom we shall go after a little time* the truly blest Pantænus, I mean, and the holy Clemens, my teacher, who was to me so greatly useful and helpful." St. Cyril of Alexandria calls him "a man admirably learned and skilful, and one that searched to the depths all the learning of the Greeks, with an exactness rarely attained before." So Theodoret says, "He surpassed all others, and *was a holy man.*" St. Jerome pronounces him the most learned of all the ancients; while Eusebius testifies to his theological attainments, and applauds him as an "incomparable master of Christian philosophy." But the rest shall be narrated by our translator, Mr. Wilson.

The following is the original Introductory Notice: —

Titus Flavius Clemens, the illustrious head of the Catechetical School at Alexandria at the close of the second century, was originally a pagan philosopher. The date of his birth is unknown. It is also uncertain whether Alexandria or Athens was his birthplace.

On embracing Christianity, he eagerly sought the instructions of its most eminent teachers; for this purpose travelling extensively over Greece, Italy, Egypt, Palestine, and other regions of the East. Only one of these teachers (who, from a reference in the *Stromata*, all appear to have been alive when he wrote) can be with certainty identified, viz., Pantænus, of whom he speaks in terms of profound reverence, and whom he describes as the greatest of them all. Returning to Alexandria, he succeeded his master Pantænus in the catechetical school, probably on the latter departing on his missionary tour to the East, somewhere about a.d. 189. He was also made a presbyter of the Church, either then or somewhat later. He continued to teach with great distinction till a.d. 202, when the persecution under Severus compelled him to retire from Alexandria. In the beginning of the reign of Caracalla we find him at Jerusalem, even then a great resort of Christian, and especially clerical, pilgrims. We also hear of him travelling to Antioch, furnished with a letter of recommendation by Alexander, bishop of Jerusalem. The close of his career is covered with obscurity. He is supposed to have died about a.d. 220.

Among his pupils were his distinguished successor in the Alexandrian school, Origen, Alexander bishop of Jerusalem, and, according to Baronius, Combefisius, and Bull, also Hippolytus.

The above is positively the sum of what we know of Clement's history.

His three great works, *The Exhortation to the Heathen* (λόγος ὁ προτρεπτικὸς πρὸς Ἕλληνας), *The Instructor, or Pædagogus* (παιδαγωγός), *The Miscellanies*, or *Stromata* (Στρωματεῖς), are among the most valuable remains of Christian antiquity, and the largest that belong to that early period.

The Exhortation, the object of which is to win pagans to the Christian faith, contains a complete and withering exposure of the abominable licentiousness, the gross imposture and sordidness of paganism. With clearness and cogency of argument, great earnestness and eloquence, Clement sets forth in contrast the truth as taught in the inspired Scriptures, the true God, and especially the personal Christ, the living Word of God, the Savior of men. It is an elaborate and masterly work, rich in felicitous classical allusion and quotation, breathing throughout the spirit of philosophy and of the Gospel, and abounding in passages of power and beauty.

The *Pædagogus, or Instructor*, is addressed to those who have been rescued from the darkness and pollutions of heathenism, and is an exhibition of Christian morals and manners, —a guide for the formation and development of

Christian character, and for living a Christian life. It consists of three books. It is the grand aim of the whole work to set before the converts Christ as the only Instructor, and to expound and enforce His precepts. In the first book Clement exhibits the person, the function, the means, methods, and ends of the Instructor, who is the Word and Son of God; and lovingly dwells on His benignity and philanthropy, His wisdom, faithfulness, and righteousness.

The second and third books lay down rules for the regulation of the Christian, in all the relations, circumstances, and actions of life, entering most minutely into the details of dress, eating, drinking, bathing, sleeping, etc. The delineation of a life in all respects agreeable to the Word, a truly Christian life, attempted here, may, now that the Gospel has transformed social and private life to the extent it has, appear unnecessary, or a proof of the influence of ascetic tendencies. But a code of Christian morals and manners (a sort of "whole duty of man" and manual of good breeding combined) was eminently needed by those whose habits and characters had been molded under the debasing and polluting influences of heathenism; and who were bound, and were aiming, to shape their lives according to the principles of the Gospel, in the midst of the all but incredible licentiousness and luxury by which society around was incurably tainted. The disclosures which Clement, with solemn sternness, and often with caustic wit, makes of the prevalent voluptuousness and vice, form a very valuable contribution to our knowledge of that period.

The full title of the *Stromata*, according to Eusebius and Photius, was Τίτου Φλαυίου Κλήμεντος τῶν κατὰ τὴν ἀληθῆ φιλοσοφίαν γνωστικῶν ὑπομνημάτων στρωματεῖς—"Titus Flavius Clement's miscellaneous collections of speculative (gnostic) notes bearing upon the true philosophy." The aim of the work, in accordance with this title, is, in opposition to Gnosticism, to furnish the materials for the construction of a true gnosis, a Christian philosophy, on the basis of faith, and to lead on to this higher knowledge those who, by the discipline of the Pædagogus, had been trained for it. The work consisted originally of eight books. The eighth book is lost; that which appears under this name has plainly no connection with the rest of the *Stromata*. Various accounts have been given of the meaning of the distinctive word in the title (Στρωματεύς); but all agree in regarding it as indicating the miscellaneous character of its contents. And they are very miscellaneous. They consist of the speculations of Greek philosophers, of heretics, and of those who cultivated the true Christian gnosis, and of quotations from sacred Scripture. The latter he affirms to be the source from which the higher Christian knowledge is to be drawn; as it was that from which the germs of truth in Plato and the Hellenic philosophy were derived. He describes philosophy as a divinely ordered preparation of the Greeks for faith in Christ, as the law was for the Hebrews; and shows the necessity and value of literature and philosophic culture for the attainment of true Christian knowledge, in opposition to the numerous body among Christians who regarded learning as useless and dangerous. He proclaims himself an eclectic, believing in the existence of fragments of truth in all systems, which may be separated from error; but declaring that the truth can be found in unity and completeness only in Christ, as it was from Him that all its scattered germs originally proceeded. The *Stromata* are written carelessly, and even confusedly; but the work is one of prodigious learning, and supplies materials of the greatest value for understanding the various conflicting systems which Christianity had to combat.

It was regarded so much as the author's great work, that, on the testimony of Theodoret, Cassiodorus, and others, we learn that Clement received the appellation of Στρωματεύς (the Stromatist). In all probability, the first part of it was given to the world about a.d. 194. The latest date to which he brings down his chronology in the first book is the death of Commodus, which happened in a.d. 192; from which Eusebius[9] concludes that he wrote this work during the reign of Severus, who ascended the imperial throne in a.d. 193, and reigned till a.d. 211. It is likely that the whole was composed ere Clement quitted Alexandria in a.d. 202. The publication of the *Pædagogus* preceded by a short time that of the *Stromata;* and the *Cohortatio* was written a short time before the *Pædagogus*, as is clear from statements made by Clement himself.

So multifarious is the erudition, so multitudinous are the quotations and the references to authors in all departments, and of all countries, the most of whose works have perished, that the works in question could only have been composed near an extensive library—hardly anywhere but in the vicinity of the famous library of Alexandria. They are a storehouse of curious ancient lore, —a museum of the fossil remains of the beauties and monstrosities of the world of pagan antiquity, during all the epochs and phases of its history. The three compositions are really parts of one whole. The central connecting idea is that of the Logos—the Word—the Son of God; whom in the first work he exhibits drawing men from the superstitions and corruptions of heathenism to faith; in the second, as training them by precepts and discipline; and in the last, as conducting them to that higher knowledge of the things of God, to which those only who devote themselves assiduously to spiritual, moral, and intellectual culture can attain. Ever before his eye is the grand form of the living personal Christ, —the Word, who "was with God, and who was God, but who became man, and dwelt among us."

Of course there is throughout plenty of false science, and frivolous and fanciful speculation.

Who is the rich man that shall be saved? (τίς ὁ σωζόμενος πλούσιος;) is the title of a practical treatise, in which Clement shows, in opposition to those who interpreted our Lord's words to the young ruler as requiring the renunciation of worldly goods, that the disposition of the soul is the great essential. Of other numerous works of Clement, of which only a few stray fragments have been preserved, the chief are the eight books of *The Hypotyposes*, which consisted of expositions of all the books of Scripture. Of these we have a few undoubted fragments. *The Adumbrations*, or *Commentaries on some of the Catholic Epistles*, and *The Selections from the Prophetic Scriptures*, are compositions of the same character, as far as we can judge, as *The Hypotyposes*, and are supposed by some to have formed part of that work.

Other lost works of Clement are: —

The Treatise of Clement, the Stromatist, on the Prophet Amos.
On Providence.
Treatise on Easter.
On Evil-speaking.
Discussion on Fasting.
Exhortation to Patience; or, To the newly baptized.
Ecclesiastical Canon; or, Against the Judaizers.
Different Terms.

The following are the names of treatises which Clement refers to as written or about to be written by him, but of which otherwise we have no trace or mention: —*On First Principles; On Prophecy; On the Allegorical Interpretation of Members and Affections when ascribed to God; On Angels; On the Devil; On the Origin of the Universe; On the Unity and Excellence of the Church; On the Offices of Bishops, Presbyters, Deacons, and Widows; On the Soul; On the Resurrection; On Marriage; On Continence; Against Heresies.*

Preserved among Clement's works is a fragment called *Epitomes of the Writings of Theodotus, and of the Eastern Doctrine*, most likely abridged extracts made by Clement for his own use, and giving considerable insight into Gnosticism.

Clement's quotations from Scripture are made from the Septuagint version, often inaccurately from memory, sometimes from a different text from what we possess, often with verbal adaptations; and not rarely different texts are blended together.

The works of Clement present considerable difficulties to the translator; and one of the chief is the state of the text, which greatly needs to be expurgated and amended. For this there are abundant materials, in the copious annotations and disquisitions, by various hands, collected together in Migne's edition; where, however, corruptions the most obvious have been allowed to remain in the text.

The publishers are indebted to Dr. W. L. Alexander for the poetical translations of the Hymns of Clement.

EXHORTATION TO THE HEATHEN

CHAPTER I.—EXHORTATION TO ABANDON THE IMPIOUS MYSTERIES OF IDOLATRY FOR THE ADORATION OF THE DIVINE WORD AND GOD THE FATHER.

Amphion of Thebes and Arion of Methymna were both minstrels, and both were renowned in story. They are celebrated in song to this day in the chorus of the Greeks; the one for having allured the fishes, and the other for having surrounded Thebes with walls by the power of music. Another, a Thracian, a cunning master of his art (he also is the subject of a Hellenic legend), tamed the wild beasts by the mere might of song; and transplanted trees—oaks—by music. I might tell you also the story of another, a brother to these—the subject of a myth, and a minstrel—Eunomos the Locrian and the Pythic grasshopper. A solemn Hellenic assembly had met at Pytho, to celebrate the death of the Pythic serpent, when Eunomos sang the reptile's epitaph. Whether his ode was a hymn in praise of the serpent, or a dirge, I am not able to say. But there was a contest, and Eunomos was playing the lyre in the summer time: it was when the grasshoppers, warmed by the sun, were chirping beneath the leaves along the hills; but they were singing not to that dead dragon, but to God All-wise, —a lay unfettered by rule, better than the numbers of Eunomos. The Locrian breaks a string. The grasshopper sprang on the neck of the instrument, and sang on it as on a branch; and the minstrel, adapting his strain to the grasshopper's song, made up for the want of the missing string. The grasshopper then was attracted by the song of Eunomos, as the fable represents, according to which also a brazen statue of Eunomos with his lyre, and the Locrian's ally in the contest, was erected at Pytho. But of its own accord it flew to the lyre, and of its own accord sang, and was regarded by the Greeks as a musical performer.

How, let me ask, have you believed vain fables and supposed animals to be charmed by music; while Truth's shining face alone, as would seem, appears to you disguised, and is looked on with incredulous eyes? And so Cithæron, and Helicon, and the mountains of the Odrysi, and the initiatory rites of the Thracians, mysteries of deceit, are hallowed and celebrated in hymns. For me, I am pained at such calamities as form the subjects of tragedy, though but myths; but by you the records of miseries are turned into dramatic compositions.

But the dramas and the raving poets, now quite intoxicated, let us crown with ivy; and distracted outright as they are, in Bacchic fashion, with the satyrs, and the frenzied rabble, and the rest of the demon crew, let us confine to Cithæron and Helicon, now antiquated.

But let us bring from above out of heaven, Truth, with Wisdom in all its brightness, and the sacred prophetic choir, down to the holy mount of God; and let Truth, darting her light to the most distant points, cast her rays all around on those that are involved in darkness, and deliver men from delusion, stretching out her very strong right hand, which is wisdom, for their salvation. And raising their eyes, and looking above, let them abandon Helicon and Cithæron, and take up their abode in Zion. "For out of Zion shall go forth the law, and the word of the Lord from Jerusalem,"—the celestial Word, the true athlete crowned in the theatre of the whole universe. What my Eunomos sings is not the measure of Terpander, nor that of Capito, nor the Phrygian, nor Lydian, nor Dorian, but the immortal measure of the new harmony which bears God's name—the new, the Levitical song.

> "Soother of pain, calmer of wrath, producing forgetfulness of all ills."

Sweet and true is the charm of persuasion which blends with this strain.

To me, therefore, that Thracian Orpheus, that Theban, and that Methymnæan,—men, and yet unworthy of the name,—seem to have been deceivers, who, under the pretence of poetry corrupting human life, possessed by a spirit of artful sorcery for purposes of destruction, celebrating crimes in their orgies, and making human woes the materials of religious worship, were the first to entice men to idols; nay, to build up the stupidity of the nations with blocks of wood and stone,—that is, statues and images,—subjecting to the yoke of extremest bondage the truly noble freedom of those who lived as free citizens under heaven by their songs and incantations. But not such is my song, which has come to loose, and that speedily, the bitter bondage of tyrannizing demons; and leading us back to the mild and loving yoke of piety, recalls to heaven those that had been cast prostrate to the earth. It alone has tamed men, the most intractable of animals; the frivolous among them answering to the fowls of the air, deceivers to reptiles, the irascible to lions, the voluptuous to swine, the rapacious to wolves. The silly are stocks and stones, and still more senseless than stones is a man who is steeped in ignorance. As our witness, let us adduce the voice of prophecy accordant with truth, and bewailing those who are crushed in ignorance and folly: "For God is able of these stones to raise up children to Abraham;" and He, commiserating their great ignorance and hardness of heart who are petrified against the truth, has raised up a seed of piety, sensitive to virtue, of those stones—of the nations, that is, who trusted in stones. Again, therefore, some venomous and false hypocrites, who plotted against righteousness, He once called "a brood of vipers." But if one of those serpents even is willing to repent, and follows the Word, he becomes a man of God.

Others he figuratively calls wolves, clothed in sheep-skins, meaning thereby monsters of rapacity in human form. And so all such most savage beasts, and all such blocks of stone, the celestial song has transformed into tractable men. "For even we ourselves were sometime foolish, disobedient, deceived, serving divers lusts and pleasures, living in malice and envy, hateful, hating one another." Thus speaks the apostolic Scripture: "But after that the kindness and love of God our savior to man appeared, not by works of righteousness which we have done, but according to His mercy, He saved us." Behold the might of the new song! It has made men out of stones, men out of beasts. Those, moreover, that were as dead, not being partakers of the true life, have come to life again, simply by becoming listeners to this song. It also composed the universe into melodious order, and tuned the discord of the elements to harmonious arrangement, so that the whole world might become harmony. It let loose the fluid ocean, and yet has prevented it from encroaching on the land. The earth, again, which had been in a state of commotion, it has established, and fixed the sea as its boundary. The violence of fire it has softened by the atmosphere, as the Dorian is blended with the Lydian strain; and the harsh cold of the air it has moderated by the embrace of fire, harmoniously arranging these the extreme tones of the universe. And this deathless strain, —the support of the whole and the harmony of all, —reaching from the centre to the circumference, and from the extremities to the central part, has harmonized this universal frame of things, not according to the Thracian music, which is like that invented by Jubal, but according to the paternal counsel of God, which fired the zeal of David. And He who is of David, and yet before him, the Word of God, despising the lyre and harp, which are but lifeless instruments, and having tuned by the Holy Spirit the universe, and especially man,—who, composed of body and soul, is a universe in miniature,—makes melody to God on this instrument of many tones; and to this instrument—I mean man—he sings accordant: "For thou art my harp, and pipe, and temple."—a harp for harmony—a pipe by reason of the Spirit—a temple by reason of the word; so that the first may sound, the second breathe, the third contain the Lord. And David the king, the harper whom we mentioned a little above, who exhorted to the truth and dissuaded from idols, was so far from celebrating demons in song, that in reality they were driven away by his music. Thus, when Saul was plagued with a demon, he cured him by merely playing. A beautiful breathing instrument of music the Lord made man, after His own image. And He Himself also, surely, who is the supramundane

Wisdom, the celestial Word, is the all-harmonious, melodious, holy instrument of God.
What, then, does this instrument—the Word of God, the Lord, the New Song—desire? To open the eyes of the blind, and unstop the ears of the deaf, and to lead the lame or the erring to righteousness, to exhibit God to the foolish, to put a stop to corruption, to conquer death, to reconcile disobedient children to their father. The instrument of God loves mankind. The Lord pities, instructs, exhorts, admonishes, saves, shields, and of His bounty promises us the kingdom of heaven as a reward for learning; and the only advantage He reaps is, that we are saved. For wickedness feeds on men's destruction; but truth, like the bee, harming nothing, delights only in the salvation of men.

You have, then, God's promise; you have His love: become partaker of His grace. And do not suppose the song of salvation to be new, as a vessel or a house is new. For "before the morning star it was;" and "in the beginning was the Word, and the Word was with God, and the Word was God." Error seems old, but truth seems a new thing.

Whether, then, the Phrygians are shown to be the most ancient people by the goats of the fable; or, on the other hand, the Arcadians by the poets, who describe them as older than the moon; or, finally, the Egyptians by those who dream that this land first gave birth to gods and men: yet none of these at least existed before the world. But before the foundation of the world were we, who, because destined to be in Him, pre-existed in the eye of God before, —we the rational creatures of the Word of God, on whose account we date from the beginning; for "in the beginning was the Word." Well, inasmuch as the Word was from the first, He was and is the divine source of all things; but inasmuch as He has now assumed the name Christ, consecrated of old, and worthy of power, he has been called by me the New Song. This Word, then, the Christ, the cause of both our being at first (for He was in God) and of our well-being, this very Word has now appeared as man, He alone being both, both God and man—the

Author of all blessings to us; by whom we, being taught to live well, are sent on our way to life eternal. For, according to that inspired apostle of the Lord, "the grace of God which bringeth salvation hath appeared to all men, teaching us, that, denying ungodliness and worldly lusts, we should live soberly, righteously, and godly, in this present world; looking for the blessed hope, and appearing of the glory of the great God and our Savior Jesus Christ."

This is the New Song, the manifestation of the Word that was in the beginning, and before the beginning. The Savior, who existed before, has in recent days appeared. He, who is in Him that truly is, has appeared; for the Word, who "was with God," and by whom all things were created, has appeared as our Teacher. The Word, who in the beginning bestowed on us life as Creator when He formed us, taught us to live well when He appeared as our Teacher; that as God He might afterwards conduct us to the life which never ends.

He did not now for the first time pity us for our error; but He pitied us from the first, from the beginning. But now, at His appearance, lost as we already were, He accomplished our salvation. For that wicked reptile monster, by his enchantments, enslaves and plagues men even till now; inflicting, as seems to me, such barbarous vengeance on them as those who are said to bind the captives to corpses till they rot together. This wicked tyrant and serpent, accordingly, binding fast with the miserable chain of superstition whomsoever he can draw to his side from their birth, to stones, and stocks, and images, and such like idols, may with truth be said to have taken and buried living men with those dead idols, till both suffer corruption together.

Therefore (for the seducer is one and the same) he that at the beginning brought Eve down to death, now brings thither the rest of mankind. Our ally and helper, too, is one and the same—the Lord, who from the beginning gave revelations by prophecy, but now plainly calls to salvation. In obedience to the apostolic injunction, therefore, let us flee from "the prince of the power of the air, the spirit that now worketh in the children of disobedience," and let us run to the Lord the savior, who now exhorts to salvation, as He has ever done, as He did by signs and wonders in Egypt and the desert, both by the bush and the cloud, which, through the favor of divine love, attended the Hebrews like a handmaid. By the fear which these inspired He addressed the hard-hearted; while by Moses, learned in all wisdom, and Isaiah, lover of truth, and the whole prophetic choir, in a way appealing more to reason, He turns to the Word those who have ears to hear. Sometimes He upbraids, and sometimes He threatens. Some men He mourns over, others He addresses with the voice of song, just as a good physician treats some of his patients with cataplasms, some with rubbing, some with fomentations; in one case cuts open with the lancet, in another cauterizes, in another amputates, in order if possible to cure the patient's diseased part or member. The Savior has many tones of voice, and many methods for the salvation of men; by threatening He admonishes, by upbraiding He converts, by bewailing He pities, by the voice of song He cheers. He spake by the burning bush, for the men of that day needed signs and wonders.

He awed men by the fire when He made flame to burst from the pillar of cloud—a token at once of grace and fear: if you obey, there is the light; if you disobey, there is the fire; but since humanity is nobler than the pillar or the bush, after them the prophets uttered their voice, —the Lord Himself speaking in Isaiah, in Elias, —speaking Himself by the mouth of the prophets. But if thou dost not believe the prophets, but supposest both the men and the fire a myth, the Lord Himself shall speak to thee, "who, being in the form of God, thought it not robbery to be equal with God, but humbled Himself,"—He, the merciful God, exerting Himself to save man. And now the Word Himself clearly speaks to thee, shaming thy unbelief; yea, I say, the Word of God became man, that thou mayest learn from man how man may become God. Is it not then monstrous, my friends, that while God is ceaselessly exhorting us to virtue, we should spurn His kindness and reject salvation?

Does not John also invite to salvation, and is he not entirely a voice of exhortation? Let us then ask him, "Who of men art thou, and whence?" He will not say Elias. He will deny that he is Christ, but will profess himself to be "a voice crying in the wilderness." Who, then, is John? In a word, we may say, "The beseeching voice of the Word crying in the wilderness." What criest thou, O voice? Tell us also. "Make straight the paths of the Lord." John is the forerunner, and that voice the precursor of the Word; an inviting voice, preparing for salvation, —a voice urging men on to the inheritance of the heavens, and through which the barren and the desolate is childless no more. This fecundity the angel's voice foretold; and this voice was also the precursor of the Lord preaching glad tidings to the barren woman, as John did to the wilderness. By reason of this voice of the Word, therefore, the barren woman bears children, and the desert becomes fruitful. The two voices which heralded the Lord's—that of the angel and that of John—intimate, as I think, the salvation in store for us to be, that on the appearance of this Word we should reap, as the fruit of this productiveness, eternal life. The Scripture makes this all clear, by referring both the voices to the same thing: "Let her hear who has not brought forth, and let her who has not had the pangs of childbirth utter her voice: for more are the children of the desolate, than of her who hath a husband."

The angel announced to us the glad tidings of a husband. John entreated us to recognize the husbandman, to seek the husband. For this husband of the barren woman, and this husbandman of the desert—who filled with divine power the barren woman and the desert—is one and the same. For because many were the children of the mother of noble rule, yet the Hebrew woman, once blessed with many children, was made childless because of unbelief: the barren woman receives the husband, and the desert the husbandman; then both become mothers through the word, the one of fruits, the other of believers. But to the unbelieving the barren and the desert are still reserved. For this reason John, the herald of the Word, besought men to make themselves ready against the coming of the Christ of God. And it was this which was signified by the dumbness of Zacharias, which waited for fruit in the person of the harbinger of Christ, that the Word, the light of truth, by becoming the Gospel, might break the mystic silence of the prophetic enigmas. But if thou desirest truly to see God, take to thyself means of purification worthy of Him, not leaves of laurel fillets interwoven with wool and purple; but wreathing thy brows with righteousness, and encircling them with the leaves of temperance, set thyself earnestly to find Christ. "For I am," He says, "the door," which we who desire to understand God must discover, that He may throw heaven's gates wide open to us. For the gates of the Word being intellectual, are opened by the key of faith. No one knows God but the Son, and he to whom the Son shall reveal Him. And I know well that He who has opened the door hitherto shut, will afterwards reveal what is within; and will show what we could not have known before, had we not entered in by Christ, through whom alone God is beheld.

CHAPTER II. —THE ABSURDITY AND IMPIETY OF THE HEATHEN MYSTERIES AND FABLES ABOUT THE BIRTH AND DEATH OF THEIR GODS.

Explore not then too curiously the shrines of impiety, or the mouths of caverns full of monstrosity, or the Thesprotian caldron, or the Cirrhæan tripod, or the Dodonian copper.

The Gerandryon, once regarded sacred in the midst of desert sands, and the oracle there gone to decay with the oak itself, consigned to the region of antiquated fables. The fountain of Castalia is silent, and the other fountain of Colophon; and, in like manner, all the rest of the springs of divination are dead, and stripped of their vainglory, although at a late date, are shown with their fabulous legends to have run dry. Recount to us also the useless oracles of that other kind of divination, or rather madness, the Clarian, the Pythian, the Didymæan, that of Amphiaraus, of Apollo, of Amphilochus; and if you will, couple with them the expounders of prodigies, the augurs, and the interpreters of dreams. And bring and place beside the Pythian those that divine by flour, and those that divine by barley, and the ventriloquists still held in honor by many. Let the secret shrines of the Egyptians and the necromancies of the Etruscans be consigned to darkness. Insane devices truly are they all of unbelieving men. Goats, too, have been confederates in this art of soothsaying, trained to divination; and crows taught by men to give oracular responses to men.

And what if I go over the mysteries? I will not divulge them in mockery, as they say Alcibiades did, but I will expose right well by the word of truth the sorcery hidden in them; and those so-called gods of yours, whose are the mystic rites, I shall display, as it were, on the stage of life, to the spectators of truth. The bacchanals hold their orgies in honor of the frenzied Dionysus, celebrating their sacred frenzy by the eating of raw flesh, and go through the distribution of the parts of butchered victims, crowned with snakes, shrieking out the name of that Eva by whom error came into the world. The symbol of the Bacchic orgies is a consecrated serpent. Moreover, according to the strict interpretation of the Hebrew term, the name Hevia, aspirated, signifies a female serpent.

Demeter and Proserpine have become the heroines of a mystic drama; and their wanderings, and seizure, and grief, Eleusis celebrates by torchlight processions. I think that the derivation of orgies and mysteries ought to be traced, the former to the wrath (ὀργή) of Demeter against Zeus, the latter to the nefarious wickedness (μύσος) relating to Dionysus; but if from Myus of Attica, who Pollodorus says was killed in hunting—no matter, I don't grudge your mysteries the glory of funeral honors. You may understand mysteria in another way, as mytheria (hunting fables), the letters of the two words being interchanged; for certainly fables of this sort hunt after the most barbarous of the Thracians, the most senseless of the Phrygians, and the superstitious among the Greeks.

Perish, then, the man who was the author of this imposture among men, be he Dardanus, who taught the mysteries of the mother of the gods, or Eetion, who instituted the orgies and mysteries of the Samothracians, or that Phrygian Midas who, having learned the cunning imposture from Odrysus, communicated it to his subjects. For I will never be persuaded by that Cyprian Islander Cinyras, who dared to bring forth from night to the light of day the lewd orgies of Aphrodité in his eagerness to deify a strumpet of his own country. Others say that Melampus the son of Amythaon imported the festivals of Ceres from Egypt into Greece, celebrating her grief in song.

These I would instance as the prime authors of evil, the parents of impious fables and of deadly superstition, who sowed in human life that seed of evil and ruin—the mysteries.

And now, for it is time, I will prove their orgies to be full of imposture and quackery. And if you have been initiated, you will laugh all the more at these fables of yours which have been held in honor. I publish without reserve what has been involved in secrecy, not ashamed to tell what you are not ashamed to worship.

There is then the foam-born and Cyprus-born, the darling of Cinyras, —I mean Aphrodité, lover of the virilia, because sprung from them, even from those of Uranus, that were cut off, —those lustful members, that, after being cut off, offered violence to the waves. Of members so lewd a worthy fruit—Aphrodité—is born. In the rites which celebrate this enjoyment of the sea, as a symbol of her birth a lump of salt and the phallus are handed to those who are initiated into the art of uncleanness. And those initiated bring a piece of money to her, as a courtesan's paramours do to her.

Then there are the mysteries of Demeter, and Zeus's wanton embraces of his mother, and the wrath of Demeter; I know not what for the future I shall call her, mother or wife, on which account it is that she is called Brimo, as is said; also the entreaties of Zeus, and the drink of gall, the plucking out of the hearts of sacrifices, and deeds that we dare not name.

Such rites the Phrygians perform in honor of Attis and Cybele and the Corybantes. And the story goes, that Zeus, having torn away the orchites of a ram, brought them out and cast them at the breasts of Demeter, paying thus a fraudulent penalty for his violent embrace, pretending to have cut out his own. The symbols of initiation into these rites, when set before you in a vacant hour, I know will excite your laughter, although on account of the exposure by no means inclined to laugh. "I have eaten out of the drum, I have drunk out of the cymbal, I have carried the Cernos, I have slipped into the bedroom." Are not these tokens a disgrace? Are not the mysteries absurdity?

What if I add the rest? Demeter becomes a mother; Core is reared up to womanhood. And, in course of time, he who begot her, —this same Zeus has intercourse with his own daughter Pherephatta, —after Ceres, the mother, —forgetting his former abominable wickedness. Zeus is both the father and the seducer of Core, and shamefully courts her in the shape of a dragon; his identity, however, was discovered. The token of the Sabazian mysteries to the initiated is "the deity gliding over the breast,"—the deity being this serpent crawling over the breasts of the initiated. Proof surely this of the unbridled lust of Zeus. Pherephatta has a child, though, to be sure, in the form of a bull, as an idolatrous poet says, —

"The bull

The dragon's father, and the father of the bull the dragon,

On a hill the herdsman's hidden ox-goad,"—

alluding, as I believe, under the name of the herdsman's ox-goad, to the reed wielded by bacchanals. Do you wish me to go into the story of Persephatta's gathering of flowers, her basket, and her seizure by Pluto (Aidoneus), and the rent in the earth, and the swine of Eubouleus that were swallowed up with the two goddesses; for which reason, in the Thesmophoria, speaking the Megaric tongue, they thrust out swine? This mythological story the women celebrate variously in different cities in the festivals called Thesmophoria and Scirophoria; dramatizing in many forms the rape of Pherephatta or Persephatta (Proserpine).

The mysteries of Dionysus are wholly inhuman; for while still a child, and the Curetes danced around [his cradle] clashing their weapons, and the Titans having come upon them by stealth, and having beguiled him with childish toys, these very Titans tore him limb from limb when but a child, as the bard of this mystery, the Thracian Orpheus, says: —

"Cone, and spinning-top, and limb-moving rattles,
And fair golden apples from the clear-toned Hesperides."

And the useless symbols of this mystic rite it will not be useless to exhibit for condemnation. These are dice, ball, hoop, apples, top, looking-glass, tuft of wool.

Athené (Minerva), to resume our account, having abstracted the heart of Dionysus, was called Pallas, from the vibrating of the heart; and the Titans who had torn him limb from limb, setting a caldron on a tripod, and throwing into it the members of Dionysus, first boiled them down, and then fixing them on spits, "held them over the fire." But Zeus having appeared, since he was a god, having speedily perceived the savor of the pieces of flesh that were being cooked, —that savor which your gods agree to have assigned to them as their perquisite, —assails the Titans with his thunderbolt, and consigns the members of Dionysus to his son Apollo to be interred. And he—for he did not disobey Zeus—bore the dismembered corpse to Parnassus, and there deposited it.

If you wish to inspect the orgies of the Corybantes, then know that, having killed their third brother, they covered the head of the dead body with a purple cloth, crowned it, and carrying it on the point of a spear, buried it under the roots of Olympus. These mysteries are, in short, murders and funerals. And the priests of these rites, who are called kings of the sacred rites by those whose business it is to name them, give additional strangeness to the tragic occurrence, by forbidding parsley with the roots from being placed on the table, for they think that parsley grew from the Corybantic blood that flowed forth; just as the women, in celebrating the Thesmophoria, abstain from eating the seeds of the pomegranate which have fallen on the ground, from the idea that pomegranates sprang from the drops of the blood of Dionysus. Those Corybantes also they call Cabiric; and the ceremony itself they announce as the Cabiric mystery.

For those two identical fratricides, having abstracted the box in which the phallus of Bacchus was deposited, took it to Etruria—dealers in honorable wares truly. They lived there as exiles, employing themselves in communicating the precious teaching of their superstition, and presenting phallic symbols and the box for the Tyrrhenians to worship. And some will have it, not improbably, that for this reason Dionysus was called Attis, because he was mutilated. And what is surprising at the Tyrrhenians, who were barbarians, being thus initiated into these foul indignities, when among the Athenians, and in the whole of Greece—I blush to say it—the shameful legend about Demeter holds its ground? For Demeter, wandering in quest of her daughter Core, broke down with fatigue near Eleusis, a place in Attica, and sat down on a well overwhelmed with grief. This is even now prohibited to those who are initiated, lest they should appear to mimic the weeping goddess. The indigenous inhabitants then occupied Eleusis: their names were Baubo, and Dusaules, and Triptolemus; and besides, Eumolpus and Eubouleus. Triptolemus was a herdsman, Eumolpus a shepherd, and Eubouleus a swineherd; from whom came the race of the Eumolpidæ and that of the Heralds—a race of Hierophants—who flourished at Athens.

Well, then (for I shall not refrain from the recital), Baubo having received Demeter hospitably, reaches to her a refreshing draught; and on her refusing it, not having any inclination to drink (for she was very sad), and Baubo having become annoyed, thinking herself slighted, uncovered her shame, and exhibited her nudity to the goddess. Demeter is delighted at the sight, and takes, though with difficulty, the draught—pleased, I repeat, at the spectacle. These are the secret mysteries of the Athenians; these Orpheus records. I shall produce the very words of Orpheus, that you may have the great authority on the mysteries himself, as evidence for this piece of turpitude: —

> "Having thus spoken, she drew aside her garments,
> And showed all that shape of the body which it is improper to name,
> And with her own hand Baubo stripped herself under the breasts.
> Blandly then the goddess laughed and laughed in her mind,
> And received the glancing cup in which was the draught."

And the following is the token of the Eleusinian mysteries: *I have fasted, I have drunk the cup; I have received from the box; having done, I put it into the basket, and out of the basket into the chest.* Fine sights truly, and becoming a goddess; mysteries worthy of the night, and flame, and the magnanimous or rather silly people of the Erechthidæ and the other Greeks besides, "whom a fate they hope not for awaits after death." And in truth against these Heraclitus the Ephesian prophesies, as "the night-walkers, the magi, the bacchanals, the Lenæn revellers, the initiated." These he threatens with what will follow death, and predicts for them fire. For what are regarded among men as mysteries, they celebrate sacrilegiously. Law, then, and opinion, are nugatory. And the mysteries of the dragon are an imposture, which celebrates religiously mysteries that are no mysteries at all, and observes with a spurious piety profane rites. What are these mystic chests? —for I must expose their sacred things, and divulge things not fit for speech. Are they not sesame cakes, and pyramidal cakes, and globular and flat cakes, embossed all over, and lumps of salt, and a serpent the symbol of Dionysus Bassareus? And besides these, are they not pomegranates, and branches, and rods, and ivy leaves? and besides, round cakes and poppy seeds? And further, there are the unmentionable symbols of Themis, marjoram, a lamp, a sword, a woman's comb, which is a euphemism and mystic expression for the *muliebria*.

O unblushing shamelessness! Once on a time night was silent, a veil for the pleasure of temperate men; but now for the initiated, the holy night is the tell-tale of the rites of licentiousness; and the glare of torches reveals vicious indulgences. Quench the flame, O Hierophant; reverence, O Torch-bearer, the torches. That light exposes Iacchus; let thy mysteries be honored, and command the orgies to be hidden in night and darkness.

The fire dissembles not; it exposes and punishes what it is bidden. Such are the mysteries of the Atheists. And with reason I call those Atheists who know not the true God, and pay shameless worship to a boy torn in pieces by the Titans, and a woman in distress, and to parts of the body that in truth cannot be mentioned for shame, held fast as they are in the double impiety, first in that they know not God, not acknowledging as God Him who truly is; the other and second is the error of regarding those who exist not, as existing and calling those gods that have no real existence, or rather no existence at all, who have nothing but a name. Wherefore the apostle reproves us, saying, "And ye were strangers to the covenants of promise, having no hope, and without God in the world."

All honor to that king of the Scythians, whoever Anacharsis was, who shot with an arrow one of his subjects who imitated among the Scythians the mystery of the Mother of the gods, as practiced by the inhabitants of Cyzicus, beating a drum and sounding a cymbal strung from his neck like a priest of Cybele, condemning him as having become effeminate among the Greeks, and a teacher of the disease of effeminacy to the rest of the Cythians.

Wherefore (for I must by no means conceal it) I cannot help wondering how Euhemerus of Agrigentum, and Nicanor of Cyprus, and Diagoras, and Hippo of Melos, and besides these, that Cyrenian of the name of Theodorus, and numbers of others, who lived a sober life, and had a clearer insight than the rest of the world into the prevailing error respecting those gods, were called Atheists; for if they did not arrive at the knowledge of the truth, they certainly suspected the error of the common opinion; which suspicion is no insignificant seed, and becomes the germ of true wisdom. One of these charges the Egyptians thus: "If you believe them to be gods, do not mourn or bewail them; and if you mourn and bewail them, do not any more regard them as gods." And another, taking an image of Hercules made of wood (for he happened most likely to be cooking something at home), said, "Come now, Hercules; now is the time to undergo for us this thirteenth labor, as you did the twelve for Eurystheus, and make this ready for Diagoras," and so cast it into the fire as a log of wood. For the extremes of ignorance are atheism and superstition, from which we must endeavor to keep. And do you not see Moses, the hierophant of the truth, enjoining that no eunuch, or emasculated man, or son of a harlot, should enter the congregation? By the two first he alludes to the impious custom by which men were deprived both of divine energy and of their virility; and by the third, to him who, in place of the only real God, assumes many gods falsely so called, —as the son of a harlot, in ignorance of his true father, may claim many putative fathers.

There was an innate original communion between men and heaven, obscured through ignorance, but which now at length has leapt forth instantaneously from the darkness, and shines resplendent; as has been expressed by one in the following lines: —

"See'st thou this lofty, this boundless ether,
Holding the earth in the embrace of its humid arms."

And in these: —

"O Thou, who makest the earth Thy chariot, and in the earth hast Thy seat,
Whoever Thou be, baffling our efforts to behold Thee."

And whatever else the sons of the poets sing.

But sentiments erroneous, and deviating from what is right, and certainly pernicious, have turned man, a creature of heavenly origin, away from the heavenly life, and stretched him on the earth, by inducing him to cleave to earthly objects. For some, beguiled by the contemplation of the heavens, and trusting to their sight alone, while they looked on the motions of the stars, straightway were seized with admiration, and deified them, calling the stars gods from their motion (θεός from θεῖν); and worshipped the sun, —as, for example, the Indians; and the moon, as the Phrygians. Others, plucking the benignant fruits of earthborn plants, called grain Demeter, as the Athenians, and the vine Dionysus, as the Thebans.

Others, considering the penalties of wickedness, deified them, worshipping various forms of retribution and calamity. Hence the Erinnyes, and the Eumenides, and the piacular deities, and the judges and avengers of crime, are the creations of the tragic poets.

And some even of the philosophers, after the poets, make idols of forms of the affections in your breasts, —such as fear, and love, and joy, and hope; as, to be sure, Epimenides of old, who raised at Athens the altars of Insult and Impudence. Other objects deified by men take their rise from events, and are fashioned in bodily shape, such as a Dike, a Clotho, and Lachesis, and Atropos, and Heimarmene, and Auxo, and Thallo, which are Attic goddesses. There is a sixth mode of introducing error and of manufacturing gods, according to which they number the twelve gods, whose birth is the theme of which Hesiod sings in his Theogony, and of whom Homer speaks in all that he says of the gods. The last mode remains (for there are seven in all)—that which takes its rise from the divine beneficence towards men. For, not understanding that it is God that does us good, they have invented saviors in the persons of the Dioscuri, and Hercules the averter of evil, and Asclepius the healer. These are the slippery and hurtful deviations from the truth which draw man down from heaven, and cast him into the abyss. I wish to show thoroughly what like these gods of yours are, that now at length you may abandon your delusion, and speed your flight back to heaven.

"For we also were once children of wrath, even as others; but God, being rich in mercy, for the great love wherewith He loved us, when we were now dead in trespasses, quickened us together with Christ." For the Word is living, and having been buried with Christ, is exalted with God. But those who are still unbelieving are called children of wrath, reared for wrath.

We who have been rescued from error, and restored to the truth, are no longer the nurslings of wrath. Thus, therefore, we who were once the children of lawlessness, have through the philanthropy of the Word now become the sons of God.

But to you a poet of your own, Empedocles of Agrigentum, comes and says: —

> "Wherefore, distracted with grievous evils,
> You will never ease your soul of its miserable woes."

The most of what is told of your gods is fabled and invented; and those things which are supposed to have taken place, are recorded of vile men who lived licentious lives: —

> "You walk in pride and madness,
> And leaving the right and straight path, you have gone away
> Through thorns and briars. Why do ye wander?
> Cease, foolish men, from mortals;
> Leave the darkness of night, and lay hold on the light."

These counsels the Sibyl, who is at once prophetic and poetic, enjoins on us; and truth enjoins them on us too, stripping the crowd of deities of those terrifying and threatening masks of theirs, disproving the rash opinions formed of them by showing the similarity of names. For there are those who reckon three Jupiters: him of Æther in Arcadia, and the other two sons of Kronos; and of these, one in Crete, and the others again in Arcadia. And there are those that reckon five Athenes: the Athenian, the daughter of Hephæstus; the second, the Egyptian, the daughter of Nilus; the third the inventor of war, the daughter of Kronos; the fourth, the daughter of Zeus, whom the Messenians have named Coryphasia, from her mother; above all, the daughter of Pallas and Titanis, the daughter of Oceanus, who, having wickedly killed her father, adorned herself with her father's skin, as if it had been the fleece of a sheep. Further, Aristotle calls the first Apollo, the son of Hephæstus and Athene (consequently Athene is no more a virgin); the second, that in Crete, the son of Corybas; the third, the son Zeus; the fourth, the Arcadian, the son of Silenus (this one is called by the Arcadians Nomius); and in addition to these, he specifies the Libyan Apollo, the son of Ammon; and to these Didymus the grammarian adds a sixth, the son of Magnes. And now how many Apollos are there? They are numberless, mortal men, all helpers of their fellow-men who similarly with those already mentioned have been so called. And what were I to mention the many Asclepiuses, or all the Mercuries that are reckoned up, or the Vulcans of fable? Shall I not appear extravagant, deluging your ears with these numerous names?

At any rate, the native countries of your gods, and their arts and lives, and besides especially their sepulchres, demonstrate them to have been men. Mars, accordingly, who by the poets is held in the highest possible honor: —

> "Mars, Mars, bane of men, blood-stained stormer of walls,"—

this deity, always changing sides, and implacable, as Epicharmus says, was a Spartan; Sophocles knew him for a Thracian; others say he was an Arcadian. This god, Homer says, was bound thirteen months: —

> "Mars had his suffering; by Alöeus' sons,
> Otus and Ephialtes, strongly bound,
> He thirteen months in brazen fetters lay."

Good luck attend the Carians, who sacrifice dogs to him! And may the Scythians never leave off sacrificing asses, as Apollodorus and Callimachus relate: —

> "Phoebus rises propitious to the Hyperboreans,
> Then they offer sacrifices of asses to him."

And the same in another place: —

> "Fat sacrifices of asses' flesh delight Phoebus."

Hephæstus, whom Jupiter cast from Olympus, from its divine threshold, having fallen on Lemnos, practiced the art of working in brass, maimed in his feet: —

> "His tottering knees were bowed beneath his weight."

You have also a doctor, and not only a brass-worker among the gods. And the doctor was greedy of gold; Asclepius was his name. I shall produce as a witness your own poet, the Boeotian Pindar: —

> "Him even the gold glittering in his hands,
> Amounting to a splendid fee, persuaded
> To rescue a man, already death's capture, from his grasp;
> But Saturnian Jove, having shot his bolt through both,
> Quickly took the breath from their breasts,
> And his flaming thunderbolt sealed their doom."

And Euripides: —

> "For Zeus was guilty of the murder of my son
> Asclepius, by casting the lightning flame at his breast."

He therefore lies struck with lightning in the regions of Cynosuris. Philochorus also says, that Poseidon was worshipped as a physician in Tenos; and that Kronos settled in Sicily, and there was buried. Patroclus the Thurian, and Sophocles the younger, in three tragedies, have told the story of the Dioscuri; and these Dioscuri were only two mortals, if Homer is worthy of credit: —

> " . . . . . . but they beneath the teeming earth,
> In Lacedæmon lay, their native land."

And, in addition, he who wrote the Cyprian poems says Castor was mortal, and death was decreed to him by fate; but Pollux was immortal, being the progeny of Mars. This he has poetically fabled. But Homer is more worthy of credit, who spoke as above of both the Dioscuri; and, besides, proved Herucles to be a mere phantom: —

> "The man Hercules, expert in mighty deeds."

Hercules, therefore, was known by Homer himself as only a mortal man. And Hieronymus the philosopher describes the make of his body, as tall, bristling-haired, robust; and Dicærchus says that he was square-built, muscular, dark, hook-nosed, with greyish eyes and long hair. This Hercules, accordingly, after living fifty-two years, came to his end, and was burned in a funeral pyre in OEta.

As for the Muses, whom Alcander calls the daughters of Zeus and Mnemosyne, and the rest of the poets and authors deify and worship, —those Muses, in honor of whom whole states have already erected museums, being handmaids, were hired by Megaclo, the daughter of Macar. This Macar reigned over the Lesbians, and was always quarrelling with his wife; and Megaclo was vexed for her mother's sake. What would she not do on her account? Accordingly she hires those handmaids, being so many in number, and calls them Mysæ, according to the dialect of the Æolians. These she taught to sing deeds of the olden time, and play melodiously on the lyre. And they, by assiduously playing the lyre, and singing sweetly to it, soothed Macar, and put a stop to his ill-temper. Wherefore Megaclo, as a token of gratitude to them, on her mother's account erected brazen pillars, and ordered them to be held in honor in all the temples. Such, then, are the Muses. This account is in Myrsilus of Lesbos.

And now, then, hear the loves of your gods, and the incredible tales of their licentiousness, and their wounds, and their bonds, and their laughings, and their fights, their servitudes too, and their banquets; and furthermore, their embraces, and tears, and sufferings, and lewd delights. Call me Poseidon, and the troop of damsels deflowered by him, Amphitrite, Amymone, Alope, Melanippe, Alcyone, Hippothoe, Chione, and myriads of others; with whom, though so many, the passions of your Poseidon were not satiated.

Call me Apollo; this is Phoebus, both a holy prophet and a good adviser. But Sterope will not say that, nor Æthousa, nor Arsinoe, nor Zeuxippe, nor Prothoe, nor Marpissa, nor

Hypsipyle. For Daphne alone escaped the prophet and seduction.

And, above all, let the father of gods and men, according to you, himself come, who was so given to sexual pleasure, as to lust after all, and indulge his lust on all, like the goats of the Thmuitæ. And thy poems, O Homer, fill me with admiration!

> "He said, and nodded with his shadowy brows;
> Waved on the immortal head the ambrosial locks,
> And all Olympus trembled at his nod."

Thou makest Zeus venerable, O Homer; and the nod which thou dost ascribe to him is most reverend. But show him only a woman's girdle, and Zeus is exposed, and his locks are dishonored. To what a pitch of licentiousness did that Zeus of yours proceed, who spent so many nights in voluptuousness with Alcmene? For not even these nine nights were long to this insatiable monster. But, on the contrary, a whole lifetime were short enough for his lust; that he might beget for us the evil-averting god.

Hercules, the son of Zeus—a true son of Zeus—was the offspring of that long night, who with hard toil accomplished the twelve labors in a long time, but in one night deflowered the fifty daughters of Thestius, and thus was at once the debaucher and the bridegroom of so many virgins. It is not, then, without reason that the poets call him a cruel wretch and a nefarious scoundrel. It were tedious to recount his adulteries of all sorts, and debauching of boys. For your gods did not even abstain from boys, one having loved Hylas, another Hyacinthus, another Pelops, another Chrysippus, and another Ganymede. Let such gods as these be worshipped by your wives, and let them pray that their husbands be such as these—so temperate; that, emulating them in the same practices, they may be like the gods. Such gods let your boys be trained to worship, that they may grow up to be men with the accursed likeness of fornication on them received from the gods.

But it is only the male deities, perhaps, that are impetuous in sexual indulgence.

"The female deities stayed each in the house, for shame," says Homer; the goddesses blushing, for modesty's sake, to look on Aphrodité when she had been guilty of adultery. But these are more passionately licentious, bound in the chains of adultery; Eos having disgraced herself with Tithonus, Selene with Endymion, Nereis with Æacus, Thetis with Peleus, Demeter with Jason, Persephatta with Adonis. And Aphrodité having disgraced herself with Ares, crossed over to Cinyra and married Anchises, and laid snares for Phaëthon, and loved Adonis. She contended with the ox-eyed Juno; and the goddesses un-robed for the sake of the apple, and presented themselves naked before the shepherd, that he might decide which was the fairest.

But come, let us briefly go the round of the games, and do away with those solemn assemblages at tombs, the Isthmian, Nemean, and Pythian, and finally the Olympian. At Pytho the Pythian dragon is worshipped, and the festival-assemblage of the serpent is called by the name Pythia. At the Isthmus the sea spit out a piece of miserable refuse; and the Isthmian games bewail Melicerta.

At Nemea another—a little boy, Archemorus—was buried; and the funeral games of the child are called Nemea. Pisa is the grave of the Phrygian charioteer, O Hellenes of all tribes; and the Olympian games, which are nothing else than the funeral sacrifices of Pelops, the Zeus of Phidias claims for himself. The mysteries were then, as is probable, games held in honor of the dead; so also were the oracles, and both became public. But the mysteries at Sagra and in Alimus of Attica were confined to Athens. But those contests and *phalloi* consecrated to Dionysus were a world's shame, pervading life with their deadly influence. For Dionysus, eagerly desiring to descend to Hades, did not know the way; a man, by name Prosymnus, offers to tell him, not without reward. The reward was a disgraceful one, though not so in the opinion of Dionysus: it was an Aphrodisian favor that was asked of Dionysus as a reward. The god was not reluctant to grant the request made to him, and promises to fulfill it should he return, and confirms his promise with an oath. Having learned the way, he departed and again returned: he did not find Prosymnus, for he had died. In order to acquit himself of his promise to his lover, he rushes to his tomb, and burns with unnatural lust. Cutting a fig-branch that came to his hand, he shaped the phallus, and so performed his promise to the dead man. As a mystic memorial of this incident, *phalloi* are raised aloft in honor of Dionysus through the various cities. "For did they not make a procession in honor of Dionysus, and sing most shameless songs in honor of the pudenda, all would go wrong," says Heraclitus. This is that Pluto and Dionysus in whose honor they give themselves up to frenzy, and play the bacchanal, —not so much, in my opinion, for the sake of intoxication, as for the sake of the shameless ceremonial practiced. With reason, therefore, such as have become slaves of their passions are your gods!

Furthermore, like the Helots among the Lacedemonians, Apollo came under the yoke of slavery to Admetus in Pheræ, Hercules to Omphale in Sardis. Poseidon was a drudge to Laomedon; and so was Apollo, who, like a good-for-nothing servant, was unable to obtain his freedom from his former master; and at that time the walls of Troy were built by them for the Phrygian. And Homer is not ashamed to speak of Athene as appearing to Ulysses with a golden lamp in her hand. And we read of Aphrodite, like a wanton serving-wench, taking and setting a seat for Helen opposite the adulterer, in order to entice him.

Panyasis, too, tells us of gods in plenty besides those who acted as servants, writing thus: —

> "Demeter underwent servitude, and so did the famous lame god;

Poseidon underwent it, and Apollo too, of the silver bow,
With a mortal man for a year. And fierce Mars
Underwent it at the compulsion of his father."

And so on.

Agreeably to this, it remains for me to bring before you those amatory and sensuous deities of yours, as in every respect having human feelings.

"For theirs was a mortal body."

This Homer most distinctly shows, by introducing Aphrodite uttering loud and shrill cries on account of her wound; and describing the most warlike Ares himself as wounded in the stomach by Diomede. Polemo, too, says that Athene was wounded by Ornytus; nay, Homer says that Pluto even was struck with an arrow by Hercules; and Panyasis relates that the beams of Sol were struck by the arrows of Hercules; and the same Panyasis relates, that by the same Hercules Hera the goddess of marriage was wounded in sandy Pylos. Sosibius, too, relates that Hercules was wounded in the hand by the sons of Hippocoon. And if there are wounds, there is blood. For the *ichor* of the poets is more repulsive than blood; for the putrefaction of blood is called *ichor*. Wherefore cures and means of sustenance of which they stand in need must be furnished. Accordingly mention is made of tables, and potations, and laughter, and intercourse; for men would not devote themselves to love, or beget children, or sleep, if they were immortal, and had no wants, and never grew old. Jupiter himself, when the guest of Lycaon the Arcadian, partook of a human table among the Ethiopians—a table rather inhuman and forbidden. For he satiated himself with human flesh unwittingly; for the god did not know that Lycaon the Arcadian, his entertainer, had slain his son (his name was Nyctimus), and served him up cooked before Zeus.

This is Jupiter the good, the prophetic, the patron of hospitality, the protector of suppliants, the benign, the author of omens, the avenger of wrongs; rather the unjust, the violator of right and of law, the impious, the inhuman, the violent, the seducer, the adulterer, the amatory. But perhaps when he was such he was a man; but now these fables seem to have grown old on our hands. Zeus is no longer a serpent, a swan, nor an eagle, nor a licentious man; the god no longer flies, nor loves boys, nor kisses, nor offers violence, although there are still many beautiful women, comelier than Leda, more blooming than Semele, and boys of better looks and manners than the Phrygian herdsman. Where is now that eagle? where now that swan? where now is Zeus himself? He has grown old with his feathers; for as yet he does not repent of his amatory exploits, nor is he taught continence. The fable is exposed before you: Leda is dead, the swan is dead. Seek your Jupiter. Ransack not heaven, but earth. The Cretan, in whose country he was buried, will show him to you, —I mean Callimachus, in his hymns: —

"For thy tomb, O king,
The Cretans fashioned!"

For Zeus is dead, be not distressed, as Leda is dead, and the swan, and the eagle, and the libertine, and the serpent. And now even the superstitious seem, although reluctantly, yet truly, to have come to understand their error respecting the Gods.

"For not from an ancient oak, nor from a rock,
But from men, is thy descent."

But shortly after this, they will be found to be but oaks and stones. One Agamemnon is said by Staphylus to be worshipped as a Jupiter in Sparta; and Phanocles, in his book of the *Brave and Fair*, relates that Agamemnon king of the Hellenes erected the temple of Argennian Aphrodite, in honor of Argennus his friend. An Artemis, named the Strangled, is worshipped by the

Arcadians, as Callimachus says in his *Book of Causes;* and at Methymna another Artemis had divine honors paid her, viz., Artemis Condylitis. There is also the temple of another Artemis—Artemis Podagra (or, the gout)—in Laconica, as Sosibius says. Polemo tells of an image of a yawning Apollo; and again of another image, reverenced in Elis, of the guzzling Apollo. Then the Eleans sacrifice to Zeus, the averter of flies; and the Romans sacrifice to Hercules, the averter of flies; and to Fever, and to Terror, whom also they reckon among the attendants of Hercules. (I pass over the Argives, who worshipped Aphrodite, opener of graves.) The Argives and Spartans reverence Artemis Chelytis, or the cougher, from κελύττειν, which in their speech signifies to cough.

Do you imagine from what source these details have been quoted? Only such as are furnished by yourselves are here adduced; and you do not seem to recognize your own writers, whom I call as witnesses against your unbelief. Poor wretches that ye are, who have filled with unholy jesting the whole compass of your life—a life in reality devoid of life!

Is not Zeus the Baldhead worshipped in Argos; and another Zeus, the avenger, in Cyprus? Do not the Argives sacrifice to Aphrodite Peribaso (the protectress), and the Athenians to Aphrodite Hetæra (the courtesan), and the Syracusans to Aphrodite Kallipygos, whom Nicander has somewhere called Kalliglutos (with beautiful rump). I pass over in silence just now Dionysus Choiropsales. The Sicyonians reverence this deity, whom they have constituted the god of the muliebria—the patron of filthiness—and religiously honor as the author of licentiousness. Such, then, are their gods; such are they also who make mockery of the gods, or rather mock and insult themselves. How much better are the Egyptians, who in their towns and villages pay divine honors to the irrational creatures, than the Greeks, who worship such gods as these?

For if they are beasts, they are not adulterous or libidinous, and seek pleasure in nothing that is contrary to nature. And of what sort these deities are, what need is there further to say, as they have been already sufficiently exposed? Furthermore, the Egyptians whom I have now mentioned are divided in their objects of worship. The Syenites worship the braizefish; and the maiotes—this is another fish—is worshipped by those who inhabit Elephantine: the Oxyrinchites likewise worship a fish which takes its name from their country. Again, the Heraclitopolites worship the ichneumon, the inhabitants of Sais and of Thebes a sheep, the Leucopolites a wolf, the Cynopolites a dog, the Memphites Apis, the Mendesians a goat. And you, who are altogether better than the Egyptians (I shrink from saying worse), who never cease laughing every day of your lives at the Egyptians, what are some of you, too, with regard to brute beasts? For of your number the Thessalians pay divine homage to storks, in accordance with ancient custom; and the Thebans to weasels, for their assistance at the birth of Hercules. And again, are not the Thessalians reported to worship ants, since they have learned that Zeus in the likeness of an ant had intercourse with Eurymedusa, the daughter of Cletor, and begot Myrmidon? Polemo, too, relates that the people who inhabit the Troad worship the mice of the country, which they call Sminthoi, because they gnawed the strings of their enemies' bows; and from those mice Apollo has received his epithet of Sminthian. Heraclides, in his work, *Regarding the Building of Temples in Acarnania*, says that, at the place where the promontory of Actium is, and the temple of Apollo of Actium, they offer to the flies the sacrifice of an ox. Nor shall I forget the Samians: the Samians, as Euphorion says, reverence the sheep.

Nor shall I forget the Syrians, who inhabit Phoenicia, of whom some revere doves, and others fishes, with as excessive veneration as the Eleans do Zeus. Well, then, since those you worship are not gods, it seems to me requisite to ascertain if those are really demons who are ranked, as you say, in this second order [next to the gods]. For if the lickerish and impure are demons, indigenous demons who have obtained sacred honors may be discovered in crowds throughout your cities: Menedemus among the Cythnians; among the Tenians, Callistagoras; among the Delians, Anius; among the Laconians, Astrabacus; at Phalerus, a hero affixed to the prow of ships is worshipped; and the Pythian priestess enjoined the Platæans to sacrifice to Androcrates and Democrates, and Cyclæus and Leuco while the Median war was at its height. Other demons in plenty may be brought to light by any one who can look about him a little.

> "For thrice ten thousand are there in the all-nourishing earth
> Of demons immortal, the guardians of articulate-speaking men."

Who these guardians are, do not grudge, O Boeotian, to tell. Is it not clear that they are those we have mentioned, and those of more renown, the great demons, Apollo, Artemis, Leto, Demeter, Core, Pluto, Hercules, and Zeus himself?

But it is from running away that they guard us, O Ascræan, or perhaps it is from sinning, as forsooth they have never tried their hand at sin themselves! In that case verily the proverb may fitly be uttered: —

> "The father who took no admonition admonishes his son."

If these are our guardians, it is not because they have any ardor of kindly feeling towards us, but intent on your ruin, after the manner of flatterers, they prey on your substance, enticed by the smoke. These demons themselves indeed confess their own gluttony, saying: —

> "For with drink-offerings due, and fat of lambs,
> My altar still hath at their hands been fed;
> Such honor hath to us been ever paid."

What other speech would they utter, if indeed the gods of the Egyptians, such as cats and weasels, should receive the faculty of speech, than that Homeric and poetic one which proclaims their liking for savory odors and cookery? Such are your demons and gods, and demigods, if there are any so called, as there are demi-asses (mules); for you have no want of terms to make up compound names of impiety.

CHAPTER III. —THE CRUELTY OF THE SACRIFICES TO THE GODS.

Well, now, let us say in addition, what inhuman demons, and hostile to the human race, your gods were, not only delighting in the insanity of men, but gloating over human slaughter, —now in the armed contests for superiority in the stadia, and now in the numberless contests for renown in the wars providing for themselves the means of pleasure, that they might be able abundantly to satiate themselves with the murder of human beings.

And now, like plagues invading cities and nations, they demanded cruel oblations. Thus, Aristomenes the Messenian slew three hundred human beings in honor of Ithometan Zeus, thinking that hecatombs of such a number and quality would give good omens; among whom was Theopompos, king of the Lacedemonians, a noble victim.

The Taurians, the people who inhabit the Tauric Chersonese, sacrifice to the Tauric Artemis forthwith whatever strangers they lay hands on their coasts who have been east adrift on the sea. These sacrifices Euripides represents in tragedies on the stage. Monimus relates, in his treatise on marvels, that at Pella, in Thessaly, a man of Achaia was slain in sacrifice to Peleus and Chiron. That the Lyctii, who are a Cretan race, slew men in sacrifice to Zeus, Anticlides shows in his *Homeward Journeys;* and that the Lesbians offered the like sacrifice to Dionysus, is said by Dosidas. The Phocæans also (for I will not pass over such as they are), Pythocles informs us in his third book, *On Concord*, offer a man as a burnt sacrifice to the Taurian Artemis.

Erechtheus of Attica and Marius the Roman sacrificed their daughters, —the former to Pherephatta, as Demaratus mentions in his first book on *Tragic Subjects;* the latter to the evil-averting deities, as Dorotheus relates in his first book of *Italian Affairs*. Philanthropic, assuredly, the demons appear, from these examples; and how shall those who revere the demons not be correspondingly pious? The former are called by the fair name of saviors; and the latter ask for safety from those who plot against their safety, imagining that they sacrifice with good omens to them, and forget that they themselves are slaying men. For a murder does not become a sacrifice by being committed in a particular spot. You are not to call it a sacred sacrifice, if one slays a man either at the altar or on the highway to Artemis or Zeus, any more than if he slew him for anger or covetousness, —other demons very like the former; but a sacrifice of this kind is murder and human butchery. Then why is it, O men, wisest of all creatures, that you avoid wild beasts, and get out of the way of the savage animals, if you fall in with a bear or lion?

". . . . . As when some travelers spies,
Coiled in his path upon the mountain side,
A deadly snake, back he recoils in haste,—
His limbs all trembling, and his cheek all pale,"

But though you perceive and understand demons to be deadly and wicked, plotters, haters of the human race, and destroyers, why do you not turn out of their way, or turn them out of yours? What truth can the wicked tell, or what good can they do any one?

I can then readily demonstrate that man is better than these gods of yours, who are but demons; and can show, for instance, that Cyrus and Solon were superior to oracular Apollo. Your Phoebus was a lover of gifts, but not a lover of men. He betrayed his friend Croesus, and forgetting the reward he had got (so careful was he of his fame), led him across the

Halys to the stake. The demons love men in such a way as to bring them to the fire [unquenchable].

But O man, who lovest the human race better, and art truer than Apollo, pity him that is bound on the pyre. Do thou, O Solon, declare truth; and thou, O Cyrus, command the fire to be extinguished. Be wise, then, at last, O Croesus, taught by suffering. He whom you worship is an ingrate; he accepts your reward, and after taking the gold plays false. "Look again to the end, O Solon." It is not the demon, but the man that tells you this. It is not ambiguous oracles that Solon utters. You shall easily take him up. Nothing but true, O Barbarian, shall you find by proof this oracle to be, when you are placed on the pyre. Whence I cannot help wondering, by what plausible reasons those who first went astray were impelled to preach superstition to men, when they exhorted them to worship wicked demons, whether it was Phoroneus or Merops, or whoever else that raised temples and altars to them; and besides, as is fabled, were the first to offer sacrifices to them. But, unquestionably, in succeeding ages men invented for themselves gods to worship. It is beyond doubt that this
Eros, who is said to be among the oldest of the gods, was worshipped by no one till Charmus took a little boy and raised an altar to him in Academia, —a thing seemlier than the lust he had gratified; and the lewdness of vice men called by the name of Eros, deifying thus unbridled lust. The Athenians, again, knew not who Pan was till Philippides told them.

Superstition, then, as was to be expected, having taken its rise thus, became the fountain of insensate wickedness; and not being subsequently checked, but having gone on augmenting and rushing along in full flood, it became the originator of many demons, and was displayed in sacrificing hecatombs, appointing solemn assemblies, setting up images, and building temples, which were in reality tombs: for I will not pass these over in silence, but make a thorough exposure of them, though called by the august name of temples; that is, the tombs which got the name of temples. But do ye now at length quite give up your superstition, feeling ashamed to regard sepulchres with religious veneration. In the temple of Athene in Larissa, on the Acropolis, is the grave of Acrisius; and at Athens, on the Acropolis, is that of Cecrops, as Antiochus says in the ninth book of his *Histories*. What of Erichthonius? Was he not buried in the temple of Polias? And Immarus, the son of Eumolpus and Daira, were they not buried in the precincts of the Elusinium, which is under the Acropolis; and the daughters of Celeus, were they not interred in Eleusis? Why should I enumerate to you the wives of the Hyperboreans? They were called Hyperoche and Laodice; they were buried in the Artemisium in Delos, which is in the temple of the Delian Apollo. Leandrius says that Clearchus was buried in Miletus, in the Didymæum. Following the Myndian Zeno, it were unsuitable in this connection to pass over the sepulchre of Leucophryne, who was buried in the temple of Artemis in Magnesia; or the altar of Apollo in Telmessus, which is reported to be the tomb of Telmisseus the seer. Further, Ptolemy the son of Agesarchus, in his first book about Philopator, says that Cinyras and the descendants of Cinyras were interred in the temple of Aphrodite in Paphos. But all time would not be sufficient for me, were I to go over the tombs which are held sacred by you. And if no shame for these audacious impieties steals over you, it comes to this, that you are completely dead, putting, as really you do, your trust in the dead.

> "Poor wretches, what misery is this you suffer?
> Your heads are enveloped in the darkness of night."

CHAPTER IV. —THE ABSURDITY AND SHAMEFULNESS OF THE IMAGES BY WHICH THE GODS ARE WORSHIPPED.

If, in addition, I take and set before you for inspection these very images, you will, as you go over them, find how truly silly is the custom in which you have been reared, of worshipping the senseless works of men's hands.

Anciently, then, the Scythians worshipped their sabers, the Arabs stones, the Persians rivers. And some, belonging to other races still more ancient, set up blocks of wood in conspicuous situations, and erected pillars of stone, which were called Xoana, from the carving of the material of which they were made. The image of Artemis in Icarus was doubtless unwrought wood, and that of the Cithæronian Here was a felled tree-trunk; and that of the Samian Here, as Æthlius says, was at first a plank, and was afterwards during the government of Proclus carved into human shape. And when the Xoana began to be made in the likeness of men, they got the name of Brete, —a term derived from Brotos (man). In Rome, the historian Varro says that in ancient times the Xoaron of Mars—the idol by which he was worshipped—was a spear, artists not having yet applied themselves to this specious pernicious art; but when art flourished, error increased. That of stones and stocks—and, to speak briefly, of dead matter—you have made images of human form, by which you have produced a counterfeit of piety, and slandered the truth, is now as clear as can be; but such proof as the point may demand must not be declined.

That the statue of Zeus at Olympia, and that of Polias at Athens, were executed of gold and ivory by Phidias, is known by everybody; and that the image of Here in Samos was formed by the chisel of Euclides, Olympichus relates in his *Samiaca*. Do not, then, entertain any doubt, that of the gods called at Athens venerable, Scopas made two of the stone called Lychnis, and Calos the one which they are reported to have had placed between them, as Polemon shows in the fourth of his books addressed to Timæus. Nor need you doubt respecting the images of Zeus and Apollo at Patara, in Lycia, which Phidias executed, as well as the lions that recline with them; and if, as some say, they were the work of Bryxis, I do not dispute, —you have in him another maker of images. Whichever of these you like, write down. Furthermore, the statues nine cubits in height of Poseidon and Amphitrite, worshipped in Tenos, are the work of Telesius the Athenian, as we are told by Philochorus. Demetrius, in the second book of his *Argolics*, writes of the image of Here in Tiryns, both that the material was pear-tree and the artist was Argus.

Many, perhaps, may be surprised to learn that the Palladium which is called the Diopetes— that is, fallen from heaven—which Diomede and Ulysses are related to have carried off from Troy and deposited at Demophoon, was made of the bones of Pelops, as the Olympian Jove of other bones—those of the Indian wild beast. I adduce as my authority Dionysius, who relates this in the fifth part of his *Cycle*. And Apellas, in the *Delphics*, says that there were two Palladia, and that both were fashioned by men. But that one may suppose that I have passed over them through ignorance, I shall add that the image of Dionysus Morychus at Athens was made of the stones called Phellata, and was the work of Simon the son of Eupalamus, as Polemo says in a letter. There were also two other sculptors of Crete, as I think: they were called Scyles and Dipoenus; and these executed the statues of the Dioscuri in Argos, and the image of Hercules in Tiryns, and the effigy of the Munychian Artemis in Sicyon. Why should I linger over these, when I can point out to you the great deity himself, and show you who he was, —whom indeed, conspicuously above all, we hear to have been considered worthy of veneration? Him they have dared to speak of as made without hands—I mean the Egyptian Serapis. For some relate that he was sent as a present by the people of Sinope to Ptolemy Philadelphus, king of the Egyptians, who won their favor by sending them corn from Egypt when they were perishing with famine; and that this idol was an image of Pluto; and Ptolemy, having received the statue, placed it on the promontory which is now called Racotis; where the temple of Serapis was held in honor, and the sacred enclosure borders on the spot; and that Blistichis the courtesan having died in Canopus, Ptolemy had her conveyed there, and buried beneath the aforementioned shrine.

Others say that the Serapis was a Pontic idol, and was transported with solemn pomp to Alexandria. Isidore alone says that it was brought from the Seleucians, near Antioch, who also had been visited with a dearth of corn, and had been fed by Ptolemy. But Athenodorns the son of Sandon, while wishing to make out the Serapis to be ancient, has somehow slipped into the mistake of proving it to be an image fashioned by human hands. He says that Sesostris the Egyptian king, having subjugated the most of the Hellenic races, on his return to Egypt brought a number of craftsmen with him. Accordingly he ordered a statue of Osiris, his ancestor, to be executed in sumptuous style; and the work was done by the artist Bryaxis, not the Athenian, but another of the same name, who employed in its execution a mixture of various materials. For he had filings of gold, and silver, and lead, and in addition, tin; and of Egyptian stones not one was wanting, and there were fragments of sapphire, and hematite, and emerald, and topaz. Having ground down and mixed together all these ingredients, he gave to the composition a blue color, whence the darkish hue of the image; and having mixed the whole with the coloring matter that was left over from the funeral of Osiris and Apis, molded the Serapis, the name of which points to its connection with sepulture and its construction from funeral materials, compounded as it is of Osiris and Apis, which together make Osirapis.

Another new deity was added to the number with great religious pomp in Egypt, and was near being so in Greece by the king of the Romans, who deified Antinous, whom he loved as Zeus loved Ganymede, and whose beauty was of a very rare order: for lust is not easily restrained, destitute as it is of fear; and men now observe the sacred nights of Antinous, the shameful character of which the lover who spent them with him knew well. Why reckon him among the gods, who is honored on account of uncleanness? And why do you command him to be lamented as a son? And why should you enlarge on his beauty? Beauty blighted by vice is loathsome. Do not play the tyrant, O man, over beauty, nor offer foul insult to youth in its bloom. Keep beauty pure, that it may be truly fair. Be king over beauty, not its tyrant. Remain free, and then I shall acknowledge thy beauty, because thou hast kept its image pure: then will I worship that true beauty which is the archetype of all who are beautiful. Now the grave of the debauched boy is the temple and town of Antinous. For just as temples are held in reverence, so also are sepulchres, and pyramids, and mausoleums, and labyrinths, which are temples of the dead, as the others are sepulchres of the gods. As teacher on this point, I shall produce to you the Sibyl prophetess: —

> "Not the oracular lie of Phoebus,
> Whom silly men called God, and falsely termed Prophet;
> But the oracles of the great God, who was not made by men's hands,
> Like dumb idols of Sculptured stone."

She also predicts the ruin of the temple, foretelling that that of the Ephesian Artemis would be engulfed by earthquakes and rents in the ground, as follows: —

> "Prostrate on the ground Ephesus shall wail, weeping by the shore,
> And seeking a temple that has no longer an inhabitant."

She says also that the temple of Isis and Serapis would be demolished and burned: —

> "Isis, thrice-wretched goddess, thou shalt linger by the streams of the Nile;
> Solitary, frenzied, silent, on the sands of Acheron."

Then she proceeds: —

> "And thou, Serapis, covered with a heap of white stones,
> Shalt lie a huge ruin in thrice-wretched Egypt."

But if you attend not to the prophetess, hear at least your own philosopher, the Ephesian Heraclitus, upbraiding images with their senselessness: "And to these images they pray, with the same result as if one were to talk to the walls of his house." For are they not to be wondered at who worship stones, and place them before the doors, as if capable of activity? They worship Hermes as a god, and place Aguieus as a doorkeeper. For if people upbraid them with being devoid of sensation, why worship them as gods? And if they are thought to be endowed with sensation, why place them before the door? The Romans, who ascribed their greatest successes to Fortune, and regarded her as a very great deity, took her statue to the privy, and erected it there, assigning to the goddess as a fitting temple—the necessary. But senseless wood and stone, and rich gold, care not a whit for either savory odor, or blood, or smoke, by which, being at once honored and fumigated, they are blackened; no more do they for honor or insult. And these images are more worthless than any animal. I am at a loss to conceive how objects devoid of sense were deified, and feel compelled to pity as miserable wretches those that wander in the mazes of this folly: for if some living creatures have not all the senses, as worms and caterpillars, and such as even from the first appear imperfect, as moles and the shrew-mouse, which Nicander says is blind and uncouth; yet are they superior to those utterly senseless idols and images. For they have some one sense, —say, for example, hearing, or touching, or something analogous to smell or taste; while images do not possess even one sense. There are many creatures that have neither sight, nor hearing, nor speech, such as the genus of oysters, which yet live and grow, and are affected by the changes of the moon. But images, being motionless, inert, and senseless, are bound, nailed, glued, —are melted, filed, sawed, polished, carved. The senseless earth is dishonored by the makers of images, who change it by their art from its proper nature, and induce men to worship it; and the makers of gods worship not gods and demons, but in my view earth and art, which go to make up images. For, in sooth, the image is only dead matter shaped by the craftsman's hand. But *we* have no sensible image of sensible matter, but an image that is perceived by the mind alone, —God, who alone is truly God.

And again, when involved in calamities, the superstitious worshippers of stones, though they have learned by the event that senseless matter is not to be worshipped, yet, yielding to the pressure of misfortune, become the victims of their superstition; and though despising the images, yet not wishing to appear wholly to neglect them, are found fault with by those gods by whose names the images are called.

For Dionysius the tyrant, the younger, having stripped off the golden mantle from the statue of Jupiter in Sicily, ordered him to be clothed in a woolen one, remarking facetiously that the latter was better than the golden one, being lighter in summer and warmer in winter. And Antiochus of Cyzicus, being in difficulties for money, ordered the golden statue of Zeus, fifteen cubits in height, to be melted; and one like it, of less valuable material, plated with gold, to be erected in place of it. And the swallows and most birds fly to these statues, and void their excrement on them, paying no respect either to Olympian Zeus, or Epidaurian Asclepius, or even to Athene Polias, or the Egyptian Serapis; but not even from them have you learned the senselessness of images. But it has happened that miscreants or enemies have assailed and set fire to temples, and plundered them of their votive gifts, and melted even the images themselves, from base greed of gain. And if a Cambyses or a Darius, or any other madman, has made such attempts, and if one has killed the Egyptian Apis, I laugh at him killing their god, while pained at the outrage being perpetrated for the sake of gain. I will therefore willingly forget such villainy, looking on acts like these more as deeds of covetousness, than as a proof of the impotence of idols. But fire and earthquakes are shrewd enough not to feel shy or frightened at either demons or idols, any more than at pebbles heaped by the waves on the shore.

I know fire to be capable of exposing and curing superstition. If thou art willing to abandon this folly, the element of fire shall light thy way. This same fire burned the temple in Argos, with Chrysis the priestess; and that of Artemis in Ephesus the second time after the Amazons. And the Capitol in Rome was often wrapped in flames; nor did the fire spare the temple of Serapis, in the city of the Alexandrians. At Athens it demolished the temple of the Eleutherian Dionysus; and as to the temple of Apollo at Delphi, first a storm assailed it, and then the discerning fire utterly destroyed it. This is told as the preface of what the fire promises. And the makers of images, do they not shame those of you who are wise into despising matter? The Athenian Phidias inscribed on the finger of the Olympian Jove, Pantarkes is beautiful. It was not Zeus that was beautiful in his eyes, but the man he loved. And Praxiteles, as Posidippus relates in his book about Cnidus, when he fashioned the statue of Aphrodite of Cnidus, made it like the form of Cratine, of whom he was enamored, that the miserable people might have the paramour of Praxiteles to worship. And when Phryne the courtesan, the Thespian, was in her bloom, all the painters made their pictures of Aphrodite copies of the beauty of Phryne; as, again, the sculptors at Athens made their Mercuries like Alcibiades. It remains for you to judge whether you ought to worship courtesans. Moved, as I believe, by such facts, and despising such fables, the ancient kings unblushingly proclaimed themselves gods, as this involved no danger from men, and thus taught that on account of their glory they were made immortal. Ceux, the son of Eolus, was styled Zeus by his wife Alcyone; Alcyone, again, being by her husband styled Hera. Ptolemy the Fourth was called Dionysus; and Mithridates of Pontus was also called Dionysus; and Alexander wished to be considered the son of Ammon, and to have his statue made horned by the sculptors—eager to disgrace the beauty of the human form by the addition of a horn. And not kings only, but

private persons dignified themselves with the names of deities, as Menecrates the physician, who took the name of Zeus. What need is there for me to instance Alexarchus? He, having been by profession a grammarian, assumed the character of the sun-god, as Aristus of Salamis relates. And why mention Nicagorus? He was a native of Zela [in Pontus], and lived in the days of Alexander. Nicagorus was styled Hermes, and used the dress of Hermes, as he himself testifies. And whilst whole nations, and cities with all their inhabitants, sinking into self-flattery, treat the myths about the gods with contempt, at the same time men themselves, assuming the air of equality with the gods, and being puffed up with vainglory, vote themselves extravagant honors. There is the case of the Macedonian
Philip of Pella, the son of Amyntor, to whom they decreed divine worship in Cynosargus, although his collar-bone was broken, and he had a lame leg, and had one of his eyes knocked out. And again that of Demetrius, who was raised to the rank of the gods; and where he alighted from his horse on his entrance into Athens is the temple of Demetrius *the Alighter;* and altars were raised to him everywhere, and nuptials with Athene assigned to him by the Athenians. But he disdained the goddess, as he could not marry the statue; and taking the courtesan Lamia, he ascended the Acropolis, and lay with her on the couch of Athene, showing to the old virgin the postures of the young courtesan.

There is no cause for indignation, then, at Hippo, who immortalized his own death. For this Hippo ordered the following elegy to be inscribed on his tomb: —

> "This is the sepulchre of Hippo, whom Destiny
> Made, through death, equal to the immortal gods."

Well done, Hippo! thou showest to us the delusion of men. If they did not believe thee speaking, now that thou art dead, let them become thy disciples. This is the oracle of Hippo; let us consider it. The objects of your worship were once men, and in process of time died; and fable and time have raised them to honor. For somehow, what is present is wont to be despised through familiarity; but what is past, being separated through the obscurity of time from the temporary censure that attached to it, is invested with honor by fiction, so that the present is viewed with distrust, the past with admiration. Exactly in this way is it, then, that the dead men of antiquity, being reverenced through the long prevalence of delusion respecting them, are regarded as gods by posterity. As grounds of your belief in these, there are your mysteries, your solemn assemblies, bonds and wounds, and weeping deities.

"Woe, woe! that fate decrees my best-belov'd,
Sarpedon, by Patroclus' hand to fall."

The will of Zeus was overruled; and Zeus being worsted, laments for Sarpedon. With reason, therefore, have you yourselves called them shades and demons, since Homer, paying Athene and the other divinities sinister honor, has styled them demons: —

"She her heavenward course pursued
To join the immortals in the abode of Jove."

How, then, can shades and demons be still reckoned gods, being in reality unclean and impure spirits, acknowledged by all to be of an earthly and watery nature, sinking downwards by their own weight, and flitting about graves and tombs, about which they appear dimly, being but shadowy phantasms? Such things are your gods—shades and shadows; and to these add those maimed, wrinkled, squinting divinities the Litæ, daughters of Thersites rather than of Zeus. So that Bion—wittily, as I think—says, How in reason could men pray Zeus for a beautiful progeny, —a thing he could not obtain for himself?

The incorruptible being, as far as in you lies, you sink in the earth; and that pure and holy essence you have buried in the grave, robbing the divine of its true nature.

Why, I pray you, have you assigned the prerogatives of God to what are no gods? Why, let me ask, have you forsaken heaven to pay divine honor to earth? What else is gold, or silver, or steel, or iron, or brass, or ivory, or precious stones? Are they not earth, and of the earth?

Are not all these things which you look on the progeny of one mother—the earth?

Why, then, foolish and silly men (for I will repeat it), have you, defaming the supercelestial region, dragged religion to the ground, by fashioning to yourselves gods of earth, and by going after those created objects, instead of the uncreated Deity, have sunk into deepest darkness?

The Parian stone is beautiful, but it is not yet Poseidon. The ivory is beautiful, but it is not yet the Olympian Zeus. Matter always needs art to fashion it, but the deity needs nothing. Art has come forward to do its work, and the matter is clothed with its shape; and while the preciousness of the material makes it capable of being turned to profitable account, it is only on account of its form that it comes to be deemed worthy of veneration. Thy image, if considered as to its origin, is gold, it is wood, it is stone, it is earth, which has received shape from the artist's hand. But I have been in the habit of walking on the earth, not of worshipping it. For I hold it wrong to entrust my spirit's hopes to things destitute of the breath of life. We must therefore approach as close as possible to the images. How peculiarly inherent deceit is in them, is manifest from their very look. For the forms of the images are plainly stamped with the characteristic nature of demons. If one go round and inspect the pictures and images, he will at a glance recognize your gods from their shameful forms: Dionysus from his robe; Hephæstus from his art; Demeter from her calamity; Ino from her head-dress; Poseidon from his trident; Zeus from the swan; the pyre indicates Heracles; and if one sees a statue of a naked woman without an inscription, he understands it to be the golden Aphrodite. Thus that Cyprian Pygmalion became enamored of an image of ivory: the image was Aphrodite, and it was nude. The Cyprian is made a conquest of by the mere shape, and embraces the image. This is related by Philostephanus. A different Aphrodite in Cnidus was of stone, and beautiful. Another person became enamored of it, and shamefully embraced the stone. Posidippus relates this. The former of these authors, in his book on Cyprus, and the latter in his book on Cnidus. So powerful is art to delude, by seducing amorous men into the pit. Art is powerful, but it cannot deceive reason, nor those who live agreeably to reason. The doves on the picture were represented so to the life by the painter's art, that the pigeons flew to them; and horses have neighed to well-executed pictures of mares. They say that a girl became enamored of an image, and a comely youth of the statue at Cnidus. But it was the eyes of the spectators that were deceived by art; for no one in his senses ever would have embraced a goddess, or entombed himself with a lifeless paramour, or become enamored of a demon and a stone. But it is with a different kind of spell that art deludes you, if it leads you not to the indulgence of amorous affections: it leads you to pay religious honor and worship to images and pictures.

The picture is like. Well and good! Let art receive its meed of praise, but let it not deceive man by passing itself off for truth. The horse stands quiet; the dove flutters not, its wing is motionless. But the cow of Dædalus, made of wood, allured the savage bull; and art having deceived him, compelled him to meet a woman full of licentious passion. Such frenzy have mischief-working arts created in the minds of the insensate. On the other hand, apes are admired by those who feed and care for them, because nothing in the shape of images and girls' ornaments of wax or clay deceives them. You then will show yourselves inferior to apes by cleaving to stone, and wood, and gold, and ivory images, and to pictures. Your makers of such mischievous toys—the sculptors and makers of images, the painters and workers in metal, and the poets—have introduced a motley crowd of divinities: in the fields, Satyrs and Pans; in the woods, Nymphs, and Oreads, and Hamadryads; and besides, in the waters, the rivers, and fountains, the Naiads; and in the sea the Nereids. And now the Magi boast that the demons are the ministers of their impiety, reckoning them among the number of their domestics, and by their charms compelling them to be their slaves. Besides, the nuptials of the deities, their begetting and bringing forth of children that are recounted, their adulteries celebrated in song, their carousals represented in comedy, and bursts of laughter over their cups, which your authors introduce, urge me to cry out, though I would fain be silent. Oh the godlessness! You have turned heaven into a stage; the Divine has become a drama; and what is sacred you have acted in comedies under the masks of demons, travestying true religion by your demon-worship [superstition].

> "But he, striking the lyre, began to sing beautifully."

Sing to us, Homer, that beautiful song

> "About the amours of Ares and Venus with the beautiful crown:
> How first they slept together in the palace of Hephæstus
> Secretly; and he gave many gifts, and dishonored the bed and chamber of king
> Hephæstus."

Stop, O Homer, the song! It is not beautiful; it teaches adultery, and we are prohibited from polluting our ears with hearing about adultery for we are they who bear about with us, in this living and moving image of our human nature, the likeness of God, —a likeness which dwells with us, takes counsel with us, associates with us, is a guest with us, feels with us, feels for us.

We have become a consecrated offering to God for Christ's sake: we are the chosen generation, the royal priesthood, the holy nation, the peculiar people, who once were not a people, but are now the people of God; who, according to John, are not of those who are beneath, but have learned all from Him who came from above; who have come to understand the dispensation of God; who have learned to walk in newness of life. But these are not the sentiments of the many; but, casting off shame and fear, they depict in their houses the unnatural passions of the demons. Accordingly, wedded to impurity, they adorn their bed-chambers with painted tablets hung up in them, regarding licentiousness as religion; and lying in bed, in the midst of their embraces, they look on that Aphrodite locked in the embrace of her paramour. And in the hoops of their rings they cut a representation of the amorous bird that fluttered round Leda, —having a strong predilection for representations of effeminacy, —and use a seal stamped with an impression of the licentiousness of Zeus. Such are examples of your voluptuousness, such are the theologies of vice, such are the instructions of your gods, who commit fornication along with you; for what one wishes, that he thinks, according to the Athenian orator. And of what kind, on the other hand, are your other images? Diminutive Pans, and naked girls, and drunken Satyrs, and phallic tokens, painted naked in pictures disgraceful for filthiness. And more than this: you are not ashamed in the eyes of all to look at representations of all forms of licentiousness which are portrayed in public places, but set them up and guard them with scrupulous care, consecrating these pillars of shamelessness at home, as if, forsooth, they were the images of your gods, depicting on them equally the postures of Philænis and the labors of Heracles. Not only the use of these, but the sight of them, and the very hearing of them, we denounce as deserving the doom of oblivion. Your ears are debauched, your eyes commit fornication, your looks commit adultery before you embrace. O ye that have done violence to man, and have devoted to shame what is divine in this handiwork of God, you disbelieve everything that you may indulge your passions, and that ye may believe in idols, because you have a craving after their licentiousness, but disbelieve God, because you cannot bear a life of self-restraint. You have hated what was better, and valued what was worse, having been spectators indeed of virtue, but actors of vice. Happy, therefore, so to say, alone are all those with one accord, —

> "Who shall refuse to look on any temples
> And altars, worthless seats of dumb stones,
> And idols of stone, and images made by hands,
> Stained with the life's-blood, and with sacrifices
> Of quadrupeds, and bipeds, and fowls, and butcheries of wild beasts."

For we are expressly prohibited from exercising a deceptive art: "For thou shalt not make," says the prophet, "the likeness of anything which is in heaven above or in the earth beneath."

For can we possibly any longer suppose the Demeter, and the Core, and the mystic Iacchus of Praxiteles, to be gods, and not rather regard the art of Leucippus, or the hands of Apelles, which clothed the material with the form of the divine glory, as having a better title to the honor? But while you bestow the greatest pains that the image may be fashioned with the most exquisite beauty possible, you exercise no care to guard against your becoming like images for stupidity. Accordingly, with the utmost clearness and brevity, the prophetic word condemns this practice: "For all the gods of the nations are the images of demons; but God made the heavens, and what is in heaven." Some, however, who have fallen into error, I know not how, worship God's work instead of God Himself, —the sun and the moon, and the rest of the starry choir, —absurdly imagining these, which are but instruments for measuring time, to be gods; "for by His word they were established, and all their host by the breath of His mouth."

Human art, moreover, produces houses, and ships, and cities, and pictures. But how shall I tell what God makes? Behold the whole universe; it is His work: and the heaven, and the sun, and angels, and men, are the works of His fingers. How great is the power of God! His bare volition was the creation of the universe. For God alone made it, because He alone is truly God. By the bare exercise of volition He creates; His mere willing was followed by the springing into being of what He willed. Consequently the choir of philosophers are in error, who indeed most nobly confess that man was made for the contemplation of the heavens, but who worship the objects that appear in the heavens and are apprehended by sight. For if the heavenly bodies are not the works of men, they were certainly created for man. Let none of you worship the sun, but set his desires on the Maker of the sun; nor deify the universe, but seek after the Creator of the universe. The only refuge, then, which remains for him who would reach the portals of salvation is divine wisdom. From this, as from a sacred asylum, the man who presses after salvation, can be dragged by no demon.

CHAPTER V.—THE OPINIONS OF THE PHILOSOPHERS RESPECTING GOD.

Let us then run over, if you choose, the opinions of the philosophers, to which they give boastful utterance, respecting the gods; that we may discover philosophy itself, through its conceit making an idol of matter; although we are able to show, as we proceed, that even while deifying certain demons, it has a dream of the truth. The elements were designated as the first principles of all things by some of them: by Thales of Miletus, who celebrated water, and Anaximenes, also of Miletus, who celebrated air as the first principle of all things, and was followed afterwards by Diogenes of Apollonia. Parmenides of Elia introduced fire and earth as gods; one of which, namely fire, Hippasus of Metapontum and Heraclitus of Ephesus supposed a divinity. Empedocles of Agrigentum fell in with a multitude, and, in addition to those four elements, enumerates disagreement and agreement. Atheists surely these are to be reckoned, who through an unwise wisdom worshipped matter, who did not indeed pay religious honor to stocks and stones, but deified earth, the mother of these, —who did not make an image of Poseidon, but revered water itself. For what else, according to the original signification, is Poseidon, but a moist substance? the name being derived from *posis* (drink); as, beyond doubt, the warlike Ares is so called, from *arsis* (rising up) and *anoeresis* (destroying). For this reason mainly, I think, many fix a sword into the ground, and sacrifice to it as to Ares. The Scythians have a practice of this nature, as Eudoxus tells us in the second book of his *Travels*. The Sauromatæ, too, a tribe of the Scythians, worship a sabre, as Ikesius says in his work on *Mysteries*.

This was also the case with Heraclitus and his followers, who worshipped fire as the first cause; for this fire others named Hephæstus. The Persian Magi, too, and many of the inhabitants of Asia, worshipped fire; and besides them, the Macedonians, as Diogenes relates in the first book of his *Persica*. Why specify the Sauromatæ, who are said by Nymphodorus, in his *Barbaric Customs*, to pay sacred honors to fire? or the Persians, or the Medes, or the Magi? These, Dino tells us, sacrifice beneath the open sky, regarding fire and water as the only images of the gods.

Nor have I failed to reveal their ignorance; for, however much they think to keep clear of error in one form, they slide into it in another.

They have not supposed stocks and stones to be images of the gods, like the Greeks; nor ibises and ichneumons, like the Egyptians; but fire and water, as philosophers. Berosus, in the third book of his *Chaldaics*, shows that it was after many successive periods of years that men worshipped images of human shape, this practice being introduced by Artaxerxes, the son of Darius, and father of Ochus, who first set up the image of Aphrodite Anaitis at Babylon and Susa; and Ecbatana set the example of worshipping it to the Persians; the Bactrians, to Damascus and Sardis.

Let the philosophers, then, own as their teachers the Persians, or the Sauromatæ, or the Magi, from whom they have learned the impious doctrine of regarding as divine certain first principles, being ignorant of the great First Cause, the Maker of all things, and Creator of those very first principles, the unbeginning God, but reverencing "these weak and beggarly elements," as the apostle says, which were made for the service of man. And of the rest of the philosophers who, passing over the elements, have eagerly sought after something higher and nobler, some have discanted on the Infinite, of whom were Anaximander of Miletus, Anaxagoras of Clazomenæ, and the Athenian Archelaus, both of whom set Mind (νοῦς) above Infinity; while the Milesian Leucippus and the Chian Metrodorus apparently inculcated two first principles—fullness and vacuity. Democritus of Abdera, while accepting these two, added to them images ει ̓́δωλα; while Alcmæon of Crotona supposed the stars to be gods, and endowed with life (I will not keep silence as to their effrontery). Xenocrates of Chalcedon indicates that the planets are seven gods, and that the universe, composed of all these, is an eighth. Nor will I pass over those of the Porch, who say that the Divinity pervades all matter, even the vilest, and thus clumsily disgrace philosophy. Nor do I think will it be taken ill, having reached this point, to advert to the Peripatetics. The father of this sect, not knowing the Father of all things, thinks that He who is called the Highest is the soul of the universe; that is, he supposes the soul of the world to be God, and so is pierced by his own sword. For by first limiting the sphere of Providence to the orbit of the moon, and then by supposing the universe to be God, he confutes himself, inasmuch as he teaches that that which is without God is God. And that Eresian Theophrastus, the pupil of Aristotle, conjectures at one time heaven, and at another spirit, to be God. Epicurus alone I shall gladly forget, who carries impiety to its full length, and thinks that God takes no charge of the world. What, moreover, of Heraclides of Pontus? He is dragged everywhere to the images—the εἴδωλα—of Democritus.

CHAPTER VI. —BY DIVINE INSPIRATION PHILOSOPHERS SOMETIMES HIT ON THE TRUTH.

A great crowd of this description rushes on my mind, introducing, as it were, a terrifying apparition of strange demons, speaking of fabulous and monstrous shapes, in old wives' talk. Far from enjoining men to listen to such tales are we, who avoid the practice of soothing our crying children, as the saying is, by telling them fabulous stories, being afraid of fostering in their minds the impiety professed by those who, though wise in their own conceit, have no more knowledge of the truth than infants. For why (in the name of truth!) do you make those who believe you subject to ruin and corruption, dire and irretrievable? Why, I beseech you, fill up life with idolatrous images, by feigning the winds, or the air, or fire, or earth, or stones, or stocks, or steel, or this universe, to be gods; and, prating loftily of the heavenly bodies in this much vaunted science of astrology, not astronomy, to those men who have truly wandered, talk of the wandering stars as gods? It is the Lord of the spirits, the Lord of the fire, the Maker of the universe, Him who lighted up the sun, that I long for. I seek after God, not the works of God. Whom shall I take as a helper in my inquiry? We do not, if you have no objection, wholly disown Plato. How, then, is God to be searched out, O Plato? "For both to find the Father and Maker of this universe is a work of difficulty; and having found Him, to declare Him fully, is impossible."

Why so? by Himself, I beseech you! For He can by no means be expressed. Well done, Plato! Thou hast touched on the truth. But do not flag. Undertake with me the inquiry respecting the Good. For into all men whatever, especially those who are occupied with intellectual pursuits, a certain divine effluence has been instilled; wherefore, though reluctantly, they confess that God is one, indestructible, unbegotten, and that somewhere above in the tracts of heaven, in His own peculiar appropriate eminence, whence He surveys all things, He has an existence true and eternal.

> "Tell me what I am to conceive God to be,
> Who sees all things, and is Himself unseen,"

Euripides says. Accordingly, Menander seems to me to have fallen into error when he said: —

> "O sun! for thou, first of gods, ought to be worshipped,
> By whom it is that we are able to see the other gods."

For the sun never could show me the true God; but that healthful Word, that is the Sun of the soul, by whom alone, when He arises in the depths of the soul, the eye of the soul itself is irradiated. Whence accordingly, Democritus, not without reason, says, "that a few of the men of intellect, raising their hands upwards to what we Greeks now call the air (ἀήρ), called the whole expanse Zeus, or God: He, too, knows all things, gives and takes away, and He is King of all."

Of the same sentiments is Plato, who somewhere alludes to God thus: "Around the King of all are all things, and He is the cause of all good things." Who, then, is the King of all? God, who is the measure of the truth of all existence. As, then, the things that are to be measured are contained in the measure, so also the knowledge of God measures and comprehends truth. And the truly holy Moses says: "There shall not be in thy bag a balance and a balance, great or small, but a true and just balance shall be to thee," deeming the balance and measure and number of the whole to be God. For the unjust and unrighteous idols are hid at home in the bag, and, so to speak, in the polluted soul. But the only just measure is the only true God, always just, continuing the self-same; who measures all things, and weighs them by righteousness as in a balance, grasping and sustaining universal nature in equilibrium. "God, therefore, as the old saying has it, occupying the beginning, the middle, and the end of all that is in being, keeps the straight course, while He makes the circuit of nature; and justice always follows Him, avenging those who violate the divine law."

Whence, O Plato, is that hint of the truth which thou givest? Whence this rich copiousness of diction, which proclaims piety with oracular utterance? The tribes of the barbarians, he says, are wiser than these; I know thy teachers, even if thou wouldst conceal them. You have learned geometry from the Egyptians, astronomy from the Babylonians; the charms of healing you have got from the Thracians; the Assyrians also have taught you many things; but for the laws that are consistent with truth, and your sentiments respecting God, you are indebted to the Hebrews,

> "Who do not worship through vain deceits
> The works of men, of gold, and brass, and silver, and ivory,
> And images of dead men, of wood and stone,
> Which other men, led by their foolish inclinations, worship;
> But raise to heaven pure arms:
> When they rise from bed, purifying themselves with water,
> And worship alone the Eternal, who reigns for ever more."

And let it not be this one man alone—Plato; but, O philosophy, hasten to produce many others also, who declare the only true God to be God, through His inspiration, if in any measure they have grasped the truth. For Antisthenes did not think out this doctrine of the Cynics; but it is in virtue of his being a disciple of Socrates that he says, "that God is not like to any; wherefore no one can know Him from an image." And

Xenophon the Athenian would have in his own person committed freely to writing somewhat of the truth, and given the same testimony as Socrates, had he not been afraid of the cup of poison, which Socrates had to drink. But he hints nothing less; he says: "How great and powerful He is who moves all things, and is Himself at rest, is manifest; but what He is in form is not revealed. The sun himself, intended to be the source of light to all around, does not deem it fitting to allow himself to be looked at; but if any one audaciously gazes on him, he is deprived of sight." Whence, then, does the son of Gryllus learn his wisdom? Is it not manifestly from the prophetess of the Hebrews who prophesies in the following style? —

> "What flesh can see with the eye the celestial,
> The true, the immortal God, who inhabits the vault of heaven?
> Nay, men born mortal cannot even stand
> Before the rays of the sun."

Cleanthes Pisadeus, the Stoic philosopher, who exhibits not a poetic theogony, but a true theology, has not concealed what sentiments he entertained respecting God: —

> "If you ask me what is the nature of the good, listen:
> That which is regular, just, holy, pious.
> Self-governing, useful, fair, fitting,
> Grave, independent, always beneficial;
> That feels no fear or grief; profitable, painless,
> Helpful, pleasant, safe, friendly;
> Held in esteem, agreeing with itself, honorable;
> Humble, careful, meek, zealous,
> Perennial, blameless, ever-during:
> Mean is every one who looks to opinion
> With the view of obtaining some advantage from it."

Here, as I think, he clearly teaches of what nature God is; and that the common opinion and religious customs enslave those that follow them, but seek not after God.

We must not either keep the Pythagoreans in the background, who say: "God is one; and He is not, as some suppose, outside of this frame of things, but within it; but, in all the entireness of His being, is in the whole circle of existence, surveying all nature, and blending in harmonious union the whole,—the author of all His own forces and works, the giver of light in heaven, and Father of all,—the mind and vital power of the whole world,—the mover of all things." For the knowledge of God, these utterances, written by those we have mentioned through the inspiration of God, and selected by us, may suffice even for the man that has but small power to examine into truth.

CHAPTER VII. —THE POETS ALSO BEAR TESTIMONY TO THE TRUTH.

Let poetry also approach to us (for philosophy alone will not suffice): poetry which is wholly occupied with falsehood—which scarcely will make confession of the truth, but will rather own to God its deviations into fable. Let whoever of those poets chooses advance first. Aratus considers that the power of God pervades all things: —

"That all may be secure,
Him ever they propitiate first and last,
Hail, Father I great marvel, great gain to man."

Thus also the Ascræan Hesiod dimly speaks of God: —

"For He is the King of all, and monarch
Of the immortals; and there is none that may vie
with Him in power."

Also on the stage they reveal the truth: —

"Look on the ether and heaven, and regard that as God,"

says Euripides. And Sophocles, the son of Sophilus, says: —

> "One, in truth, one is God,
> Who made both heaven and the far-stretching earth,
> And ocean's blue wave, and the mighty winds;
> But many of us mortals, deceived in heart,
> Have set up for ourselves, as a consolation in our afflictions, Images of the gods of stone, or wood, or brass, or gold, or ivory; and, appointing to those sacrifices and vain festal assemblages, are accustomed thus to practice religion."

In this venturous manner has he on the stage brought truth before the spectators. But the Thracian Orpheus, the son of OEagrus, hierophant and poet at once, after his exposition of the orgies, and his theology of idols, introduces a palinode of truth with true solemnity, though tardily singing the strain: —

> "I shall utter to whom it is lawful; but let the doors be closed, nevertheless, against all the profane. But do thou hear, O Musæus, offspring of the light-bringing moon, for I will declare what is true. And let not these things which once appeared in your breast rob you of dear life; but looking to the divine word, apply yourself to it, keeping right *the seat of intellect and feeling;* and walk well in the straight path, and to the immortal King of the universe alone direct your gaze."

Then proceeding, he clearly adds: —

> "He is one, self-proceeding; and from Him alone all things proceed, and in them He Himself exerts his activity: no mortal beholds Him, but He beholds all."

Thus far Orpheus at last understood that he had been in error: —

> "But linger no longer, O man, endued with varied wisdom; but turn and retrace your steps, and propitiate God."

For if, at the most, the Greeks, having received certain scintillations of the divine word, have given forth some utterances of truth, they bear indeed witness that the force of truth is not hidden, and at the same time expose their own weakness in not having arrived at the end. For I think it has now become evident to all, that those who do or speak aught without the word of truth are like people compelled to walk without feet. Let the strictures on your gods, which the poets, impelled by the force of truth, introduce in their comedies, shame you into salvation. Menander, for instance, the comic poet, in his drama of the *Charioteer,* says: —

> "No God pleases me that goes about
> with an old woman, and enters houses
> carrying a trencher."

For such are the begging priests of Cybele. Hence Antisthenes replies appropriately to their request for alms: —

> "I do not maintain the mother of the gods,
> for the gods maintain her."

Again, the same writer of comedy, expressing his dissatisfaction with the common usages, tries to expose the impious arrogance of the prevailing error in the drama of the *Priestess,* sagely declaring: —

> "If a man drags the Deity
> Whither he will by the sound of cymbals,

He that does this is greater than the Deity;
But these are the instruments of audacity and means of living Invented by men."

And not only Menander, but Homer also, and Euripides, and other poets in great numbers, expose your gods, and are wont to rate them, and that soundly too. For instance, they call Aphrodite dog-fly, and Hephæstus a cripple. Helen says to Aphrodite: —

"Thy godship abdicate!
Renounce Olympus!"

And of Dionysus, Homer writes without reserve: —

"He, mid their frantic orgies, in the groves
Of lovely Nyssa, put to shameful rout
The youthful Bacchus' nurses; they in fear,
Dropped each her thyrsus, scattered by the hand
Of fierce Lycurgus, with an ox-goad armed."

Worthy truly of the Socratic school is Euripides, who fixes his eye on truth, and despises the spectators of his plays. On one occasion, Apollo,

"Who inhabits the sanctuary that is in the middle of the earth,
Dispensing most certain oracles to mortals,"

is thus exposed: —

"It was in obedience to him that I killed her who brought me forth;
Him do you regard as stained with guilt—put him to death;
It was he that sinned, not I, uninstructed as I was
In right and justice."

He introduces Heracles, at one time mad, at another drunk and gluttonous. How should he not so represent the god who, when entertained as a guest, ate green figs to flesh, uttering discordant howls, that even his barbarian host remarked it? In his drama of *Ion,* too, he barefacedly brings the gods on the stage: —

> "How, then, is it right for you, who have given laws to mortals,
> To be yourselves guilty of wrong?
> And if—what will never take place, yet I will state the supposition—
> You will give satisfaction to men for your adulteries,
> You, Poseidon, and you, Zeus, the ruler of heaven, —
> You will, in order to make recompense for your misdeeds,
> Have to empty your temples."

CHAPTER VIII. —THE TRUE DOCTRINE IS TO BE SOUGHT IN THE PROPHETS.

It is now time, as we have dispatched in order the other points, to go to the prophetic Scriptures; for the oracles present us with the appliances necessary for the attainment of piety, and so establish the truth. The divine Scriptures and institutions of wisdom form the short road to salvation. Devoid of embellishment, of outward beauty of diction, of wordiness and seductiveness, they raise up humanity strangled by wickedness, teaching men to despise the casualties of life; and with one and the same voice remedying many evils, they at once dissuade us from pernicious deceit, and clearly exhort us to the attainment of the salvation set before us. Let the Sibyl prophetess, then, be the first to sing to us the song of salvation: —

> "So He is all sure and unerring:
> Come, follow no longer darkness and gloom;

See, the sun's sweet-glancing light shines gloriously.
Know, and lay up wisdom in your hearts:
There is one God, who sends rains, and winds, and earthquakes,
Thunderbolts, famines, plagues, and dismal sorrows,
And snows and ice. But why detail particulars?
He reigns over heaven, He rules earth,
He truly is;"—

where, in remarkable accordance with inspiration she compares delusion to darkness, and the knowledge of God to the sun and light, and subjecting both to comparison, shows the choice we ought to make. For falsehood is not dissipated by the bare presentation of the truth, but by the practical improvement of the truth it is ejected and put to flight.

Jeremiah the prophet, gifted with consummate wisdom, or rather the Holy Spirit in Jeremiah, exhibits God. "Am I a God at hand," he says, "and not a God afar off? Shall a man do ought in secret, and I not see him? Do I not fill heaven and earth? Saith the Lord."

And again by Isaiah, "Who shall measure heaven with a span, and the whole earth with his hand?" Behold God's greatness, and be filled with amazement. Let us worship Him of whom the prophet says, "Before Thy face the hills shall melt, as wax melteth before the fire!" This, says he, is the God "whose throne is heaven, and His footstool the earth; and if He open heaven, quaking will seize thee." Will you hear, too, what this prophet says of idols? "And they shall be made a spectacle of in the face of the sun, and their carcasses shall be meat for the fowls of heaven and the wild beasts of the earth; and they shall putrefy before the sun and the moon, which they have loved and served; and their city shall be burned down." He says, too, that the elements and the world shall be destroyed. "The earth," he says, "shall grow old, and the heaven shall pass away; but the word of the Lord endureth forever." What, then, when again God wishes to show Himself by Moses: "Behold ye, behold ye, that I Am, and there is no other God beside Me. I will kill, and I will make to live; I will strike, and I will heal; and there is none who shall deliver out of My hands." But do you wish to hear another seer? You have the whole prophetic choir, the associates of Moses. What the Holy Spirit says by Hosea, I will not shrink from quoting: "Lo, I am He that appointeth the thunder, and createth spirit; and His hands have established the host of heaven." And once more by Isaiah. And this utterance I will repeat: "I am," he says, "I am the Lord; I who speak righteousness, announce truth. Gather yourselves together, and come. Take counsel together, ye that are saved from the nations. They have not known, they who set up the block of wood, their carved work, and pray to gods who will not save them." Then proceeding: "I am God, and there is not beside Me a just God, and a Savior: there is none except Me. Turn to Me, and ye will be saved, ye that are from the end of the earth. I am God, and there is no other; by Myself I swear." But against the worshippers of idols he is exasperated, saying, "To whom will ye liken the Lord, or to what likeness will ye compare Him? Has not the artificer made the image, or the goldsmith melted the gold and plated it with gold?"—and so on. Be not therefore idolaters, but even now beware of the threatenings; "for the graven images and the works of men's hands shall wail, or rather they that trust in them," for matter is devoid of sensation. Once more he says, "The Lord will shake the cities that are inhabited, and grasp the world in His hand like a nest." Why repeat to you the mysteries of wisdom, and sayings from the writings of the son of the Hebrews, the master of wisdom? "The Lord created me the beginning of His ways, in order to His works." And, "The Lord giveth wisdom, and from His face proceed knowledge and understanding." "How long wilt thou lie in bed, O sluggard; and when wilt thou be aroused from sleep?" "but if thou show thyself no sluggard, as a fountain thy harvest shall come," the "Word of the Father, the benign light, the Lord that bringeth light, faith to all, and salvation." For "the Lord who created the earth by His power," as Jeremiah says, "has raised up the world by His wisdom;" for wisdom, which is His word, raises us up to the truth, who have fallen prostrate before idols, and is itself the first resurrection from our fall. Whence Moses, the man of God, dissuading from all idolatry, beautifully exclaims, "Hear, O Israel, the Lord thy God is one Lord; and thou shall worship the Lord thy God, and Him only shall thou serve." "Now therefore be wise, O men," according to that blessed psalmist David; "lay hold on instruction, lest the Lord be angry, and ye perish from the way of righteousness, when His wrath has quickly kindled. Blessed are all they who put their trust in Him." But already the Lord, in His surpassing pity, has inspired the song of salvation, sounding like a battle march, "Sons of men, how long will ye be slow of heart? Why do you love vanity, and seek after a lie?" What, then, is the vanity, and what the lie? The holy apostle of the Lord, reprehending the Greeks, will show thee: "Because that, when they knew God, they glorified Him not as God, neither were thankful; but became vain in their imaginations, and changed the glory of God into the likeness of corruptible man, and worshipped and served the creature more than the Creator." And verily this is the God who "in the beginning made the heaven and the earth." But you do not know God, and worship the heaven, and how shall you escape the guilt of impiety? Hear again the prophet speaking: "The sun, shall suffer eclipse, and the heaven be darkened; but the Almighty shall shine for ever: while the powers of the heavens shall be shaken, and the heavens stretched out and drawn together shall be rolled as a parchment-skin (for these are the prophetic expressions), and the earth shall flee away from before the face of the Lord."

CHAPTER IX. — "THAT THOSE GRIEVOUSLY SIN WHO DESPISE OR NEGLECT GOD'S GRACIOUS CALLING."

I could adduce ten thousand Scriptures of which not "one tittle shall pass away," without being fulfilled; for the mouth of the Lord the Holy Spirit hath spoken these things.

"Do not any longer," he says, "my son, despise the chastening of the Lord, nor faint when thou art rebuked of Him." O surpassing love for man! Not as a teacher speaking to his pupils, not as a master to his domestics, nor as God to men, but as a father, does the Lord gently admonish his children. Thus Moses confesses that "he was filled with quaking and terror" while he listened to God speaking concerning the Word. And art not thou afraid as thou hearest the voice of the Divine Word? Art not thou distressed? Do you not fear, and hasten to learn of Him, —that is, to salvation, —dreading wrath, loving grace, eagerly striving after the hope set before us, that you may shun the judgment threatened? Come, come, O my young people! For if you become not again as little children, and be born again, as saith the Scripture, you shall not receive the truly existent Father, nor shall you ever enter into the kingdom of heaven. For in what way is a stranger permitted to enter? Well, as I take it, then, when he is enrolled and made a citizen, and receives one to stand to him in the relation of father, then will he be occupied with the Father's concerns, then shall he be deemed worthy to be made His heir, then will he share the kingdom of the Father with His own dear Son. For this is the first-born Church, composed of many good children; these are "the firstborn enrolled in heaven, who hold high festival with so many myriads of angels." We, too, are first-born sons, who are reared by God, who are the genuine friends of the First-born, who first of all other men attained to the knowledge of God, who first were wrenched away from our sins, first severed from the devil. And now the more benevolent God is, the more impious men are; for He desires us from slaves to become sons, while they scorn to become sons. O the prodigious folly of being ashamed of the Lord! He offers freedom, you flee into bondage; He bestows salvation, you sink down into destruction; He confers everlasting life, you wait for punishment, and prefer the fire which the Lord "has prepared for the devil and his angels." Wherefore the blessed apostle says: "I testify in the Lord, that ye walk no longer as the

Gentiles walk, in the vanity of their mind; having their understanding darkened, being alienated from the life of God through the ignorance that is in them, because of the hardness of their heart: who, being past feeling, have given themselves over to lasciviousness, to work all uncleanness and concupiscence." After the accusation of such a witness, and his invocation of God, what else remains for the unbelieving than judgment and condemnation? And the Lord, with ceaseless assiduity, exhorts, terrifies, urges, rouses, admonishes; He awakes from the sleep of darkness, and raises up those who have wandered in error. "Awake," He says, "thou that sleepest, and arise from the dead, and Christ shall give thee light,"—Christ, the Sun of the Resurrection, He "who was born before the morning star," and with His beams bestows life. Let no one then despise the Word, lest he unwittingly despise himself. For the Scripture somewhere says, "To-day, if ye will hear His voice, harden not your hearts, as in the provocation, in the day of temptation in the wilderness, when your fathers proved Me by trial." And what was the trial? If you wish to learn, the Holy Spirit will show you: "And saw my works," He says, "forty years. Wherefore I was grieved with that generation, and said, They do always err in heart, and have not known My ways. So I sware in my wrath, they shall not enter into My rest." Look to the threatening! Look to the exhortation! Look to the punishment! Why, then, should we any longer change grace into wrath, and not receive the word with open ears, and entertain God as a guest in pure spirits? For great is the grace of His promise, "if to-day we hear His voice." And that to-day is lengthened out day by day, while it is called today. And to the end the today and the instruction continue; and then the true today, the never-ending day of God, extends over eternity. Let us then ever obey the voice of the divine word. For the today signifies eternity. And day is the symbol of light; and the light of men is the Word, by whom we behold God. Rightly, then, to those that have believed and obey, grace will superabound; while with those that have been unbelieving, and err in heart, and have not known the Lord's ways, which John commanded to make straight and to prepare, God is incensed, and those He threatens. And, indeed, the old Hebrew wanderers in the desert received typically the end of the threatening; for they are said not to have entered into the rest, because of unbelief, till, having followed the successor of Moses, they learned by experience, though late, that they could not be saved otherwise than by believing on Jesus. But the Lord, in His love to man, invites all men to the knowledge of the truth, and for this end sends the Paraclete. What, then, is this knowledge? Godliness; and "godliness," according to Paul, "is profitable for all things, having the promise of the life that now is, and of that which is to come." If eternal salvation were to be sold, for how much, O men, would you propose to purchase it? Were one to estimate the value of the whole of Pactolus, the fabulous river of gold, he would not have reckoned up a price equivalent to salvation.

Do not, however, faint. You may, if you choose, purchase salvation, though of inestimable value, with your own resources, love and living faith, which will be reckoned a suitable price. This recompense God cheerfully accepts; "for we trust in the living God, who is the Savior of all men, especially of those who believe."

But the rest, round whom the world's growths have fastened, as the rocks on the seashore are covered over with sea-weed, make light of immortality, like the old man of Ithaca, eagerly longing to see, not the truth, not the fatherland in heaven, not the true light, but smoke. But godliness, that makes man as far as can be like God, designates God as our suitable teacher, who alone can worthily assimilate man to God. This teaching the apostle knows as truly divine. "Thou, O Timothy," he says, "from a child hast known the holy letters, which are able to make thee wise unto salvation, through faith that is in Christ Jesus." For truly holy are those letters that sanctify and deify; and the writings or volumes that consist of those holy letters and syllables, the same apostle consequently calls "inspired of God, being profitable for doctrine, for reproof, for correction, for instruction in righteousness, that the man of God may be perfect, thoroughly furnished to every good work." No one will be so impressed by the exhortations of any of the saints, as he is by the words of the Lord Himself, the lover of man. For this, and nothing but this, is His only work—the salvation of man. Therefore He Himself, urging them on to salvation, cries, "The kingdom of heaven is at hand." Those men that draw near through fear, He converts. Thus also the apostle of the Lord, beseeching the Macedonians, becomes the interpreter of the divine voice, when he says, "The Lord is at hand; take care that ye be not apprehended empty." But are ye so devoid of fear, or rather of faith, as not to believe the Lord Himself, or Paul, who in Christ's stead thus entreats: "Taste and see that Christ is God?" Faith will lead you in; experience will teach you; Scripture will train you, for it says, "Come hither, O children; listen to me, and I will teach you the fear of the Lord." Then, as to those who already believe, it briefly adds, "What man is he that desireth life, that loveth to see good days?" It is we, we shall say—we who are the devotees of good, we who eagerly desire good things. Hear, then, ye who are far off, hear ye who are near: the word has not been hidden from any; light is common, it shines "on all men." No one is a Cimmerian in respect to the word. Let us haste to salvation, to regeneration; let us who are many haste that we may be brought together into one love, according to the union of the essential unity; and let us, by being made good, conformably follow after union, seeking after the good Monad. The union of many in one, issuing in the production of divine harmony out of a medley of sounds and division, becomes one symphony following one choir-leader and teacher, the Word, reaching and resting in the same truth, and crying Abba, Father. This, the true utterance of His children, God accepts with gracious welcome—the first-fruits He receives from them.

CHAPTER X.—ANSWER TO THE OBJECTION OF THE HEATHEN, THAT IT WAS NOT RIGHT TO ABANDON THE CUSTOMS OF THEIR FATHERS.

But you say it is not creditable to subvert the customs handed down to us from our fathers. And why, then, do we not still use our first nourishment, milk, to which our nurses accustomed us from the time of our birth? Why do we increase or diminish our patrimony, and not keep it exactly the same as we got it? Why do we not still vomit on our parents' breasts, or still do the things for which, when infants, and nursed by our mothers, we were laughed at, but have corrected ourselves, even if we did not fall in with good instructors? Then, if excesses in the indulgence of the passions, though pernicious and dangerous, yet are accompanied with pleasure, why do we not in the conduct of life abandon that usage which is evil, and provocative of passion, and godless, even should our fathers feel hurt, and betake ourselves to the truth, and seek Him who is truly our Father, rejecting custom as a deleterious drug? For of all that I have undertaken to do, the task I now attempt is the noblest, viz., to demonstrate to you how inimical this insane and most wretched custom is to godliness. For a boon so great, the greatest ever given by God to the human race, would never have been hated and rejected, had not you been carried away by custom, and then shut your ears against us; and just as unmanageable horses throw off the reins, and take the bit between their teeth, you rush away from the arguments addressed to you, in your eager desire to shake yourselves clear of us, who seek to guide the chariot of your life, and, impelled by your folly, dash towards the precipices of destruction, and regard the holy word of God as an accursed thing. The reward of your choice, therefore, as described by Sophocles, follows: —

"The mind a blank, useless ears, vain thoughts."

And you know not that, of all truths, this is the truest, that the good and godly shall obtain the good reward, inasmuch as they held goodness in high esteem; while, on the other hand, the wicked shall receive meet punishment. For the author of evil, torment has been prepared; and so the prophet Zecharias threatens him: "He that hath chosen Jerusalem rebuke thee; lo, is not this a brand plucked from the fire?" What an infatuated desire, then, for voluntary death is this, rooted in men's minds! Why do they flee to this fatal brand, with which they shall be burned, when it is within their power to live nobly according to God, and not according to custom? For God bestows life freely; but evil custom, after our departure from this world, brings on the sinner unavailing remorse with punishment. *By sad experience, even a child knows* how superstition destroys and piety saves. Let any of you look at those who minister before the idols, their hair matted, their persons disgraced with filthy and tattered clothes; who never come near a bath, and let their nails grow to an extraordinary length, like wild beasts; many of them castrated, who show the idol's temples to be in reality graves or prisons. These appear to me to bewail the gods, not to worship them, and their sufferings to be worthy of pity rather than piety. And seeing these things, do you still continue blind, and will you not look up to the Ruler of all, the Lord of the universe? And will you not escape from those dungeons, and flee to the mercy that comes down from heaven? For God, of His great love to man, comes to the help of man, as the mother-bird flies to one of her young that has fallen out of the nest; and if a serpent open its mouth to swallow the little bird, "the mother flutters round, uttering cries of grief over her dear progeny;" and God the Father seeks His creature, and heals his transgression, and pursues the serpent, and recovers the young one, and incites it to fly up to the nest.

Thus dogs that have strayed, track out their master by the scent; and horses that have thrown their riders, come to their master's call if he but whistle. "The ox," it is said, "knoweth his owner, and the ass his master's crib; but Israel hath not known Me." What, then, of the Lord? He remembers not our ill desert; He still pities, He still urges us to repentance.

And I would ask you, if it does not appear to you monstrous, that you men who are God's handiwork, who have

received your souls from Him, and belong wholly to God, should be subject to another master, and, what is more, serve the tyrant instead of the rightful King—the evil one instead of the good? For, in the name of truth, what man in his senses turns his back on good, and attaches himself to evil? What, then, is he who flees from God to consort with demons? Who, that may become a son of God, prefers to be in bondage?
Or who is he that pursues his way to Erebus, when it is in his power to be a citizen of heaven, and to cultivate Paradise, and walk about in heaven and partake of the tree of life and immortality, and, cleaving his way through the sky in the track of the luminous cloud, behold, like Elias, the rain of salvation? Some there are, who, like worms wallowing in marshes and mud in the streams of pleasure, feed on foolish and useless delights—swinish men. For swine, it is said, like mud better than pure water; and, according to Democritus, "doat upon dirt."

Let us not then be enslaved or become swinish; but, as true children of the light, let us raise our eyes and look on the light, lest the Lord discover us to be spurious, as the sun does the eagles. Let us therefore repent, and pass from ignorance to knowledge, from foolishness to wisdom, from licentiousness to self-restraint, from unrighteousness to righteousness, from godlessness to God. It is an enterprise of noble daring to take our way to God; and the enjoyment of many other good things is within the reach of the lovers of righteousness, who pursue eternal life, specially those things to which God Himself alludes, speaking by Isaiah: "There is an inheritance for those who serve the Lord." Noble and desirable is this inheritance: not gold, not silver, not raiment, which the moth assails, and things of earth which are assailed by the robber, whose eye is dazzled by worldly wealth; but it is that treasure of salvation to which we must hasten, by becoming lovers of the Word. Thence praise-worthy works descend to us, and fly with us on the wing of truth. This is the inheritance with which the eternal covenant of God invests us, conveying the everlasting gift of grace; and thus our loving Father—the true Father—ceases not to exhort, admonish, train, love us. For He ceases not to save, and advises the best course: "Become righteous," says the Lord. Ye that thirst, come to the water; and ye that have no money, come, and buy and drink without money. He invites to the laver, to salvation, to illumination, all but crying out and saying, The land I give thee, and the sea, my child, and heaven too; and all the living creatures in them I freely bestow upon thee. Only, O child, thirst for thy Father; God shall be revealed to thee without price; the truth is not made merchandise of. He gives thee all creatures that fly and swim, and those on the land. These the Father has created for thy thankful enjoyment. What the bastard, who is a son of perdition, foredoomed to be the slave of mammon, has to buy for money, He assigns to thee as thine own, even to His own son who loves the Father; for whose sake He still works, and to whom alone He promises, saying, "The land shall not be sold in perpetuity," for it is not destined to corruption. "For the whole land is mine;" and it is thine too, if thou receive God. Wherefore the Scripture, as might have been expected, proclaims good news to those who have believed. "The saints of the Lord shall inherit the glory of God and His power." What glory, tell me, O blessed One, which "eye hath not seen, nor ear heard, nor hath it entered into the heart of man;" and "they shall be glad in the kingdom of their Lord for ever and ever! Amen." You have, O men, the divine promise of grace; you have heard, on the other hand, the threatening of punishment: by these the Lord saves, teaching men by fear and grace. Why do we delay? Why do we not shun the punishment? Why do we not receive the free gift? Why, in fine, do we not choose the better part, God instead of the evil one, and prefer wisdom to idolatry, and take life in exchange for death? "Behold," He says, "I have set before your face death and life." The Lord tries you, that "you may choose life." He counsels you as a father to obey God. "For if ye hear Me," He says, "and be willing, ye shall eat the good things of the land:" this is the grace attached to obedience. "But if ye obey

Me not, and are unwilling, the sword and fire shall devour you:" this is the penalty of disobedience. For the mouth of the Lord—the law of truth, the word of the Lord—hath spoken these things. Are you willing that I should be your good counselor? Well, do you hear. I, if possible, will explain. You ought, O men, when reflecting on the Good, to have brought forward a witness inborn and competent, viz., faith, which of itself, and from its own resources, chooses at once what is best, instead of occupying yourselves in painfully inquiring whether what is best ought to be followed. For, allow me to tell you, you ought to doubt whether you should get drunk, but you get drunk before reflecting on the matter; and whether you ought to do an injury, but you do injury with the utmost readiness. The only thing you make the subject of question is, whether God should be worshipped, and whether this wise God and Christ should be followed: and this you think requires deliberation and doubt, and know not what is worthy of God. Have faith in us, as you have in drunkenness, that you may be wise; have faith in us, as you have in injury, that you may live. But if, acknowledging the conspicuous trustworthiness of the virtues, you wish to trust them, come and I will set before you in abundance, materials of persuasion respecting the Word. But do you—for your ancestral customs, by which your minds are preoccupied, divert you from the truth, —do you now hear what is the real state of the case as follows.

And let not any shame of this name preoccupy you, which does great harm to men, and seduces them from salvation. Let us then openly strip for the contest, and nobly strive in the arena of truth, the holy Word being the judge, and the Lord of the universe prescribing the contest. For 'tis no insignificant prize, the guerdon of immortality which is set before us. Pay no more regard, then, if you are rated by some of the low rabble who lead the dance of impiety, and are driven on to the same pit by their folly and insanity, makers of idols and worshippers of stones. For these have dared to deify men, —Alexander of Macedon, for example, whom they canonized as the thirteenth god, whose pretensions Babylon confuted, which showed him dead. I admire, therefore, the divine sophist. Theocritus was his name. After Alexander's death, Theocritus, holding up the vain opinions entertained by men respecting the gods, to ridicule before his fellow-citizens, said: "Men, keep up your hearts as long as you see the gods dying sooner than men." And, truly, he who worships gods that are visible, and the promiscuous rabble of creatures begotten and born, and attaches himself to them, is a far more wretched object than the very demons. For God is by no manner of means unrighteous, as the demons are, but in the very highest degree righteous; and nothing more resembles God than one of us when he becomes righteous in the highest possible degree: —

> "Go into the way, the whole tribe of you handicrafts-men,
> Who worship Jove's fierce-eyed daughter, the working goddess,
> With fans duly placed, fools that ye are"—

fashioners of stones, and worshippers of them. Let your Phidias, and Polycletus, and your Praxiteles and Apelles too, come, and all that are engaged in mechanical arts, who, being themselves of the earth, are workers of the earth. "For then," says a certain prophecy, "the affairs here turn out unfortunately, when men put their trust in images." Let the meaner artists, too—for I will not stop calling—come. None of these ever made a breathing image, or out of earth molded soft flesh. Who liquefied the marrow? or who solidified the bones? Who stretched the nerves? who distended the veins? Who poured the blood into them? Or who spread the skin? Who ever could have made eyes capable of seeing? Who breathed spirit into the lifeless form? Who bestowed righteousness? Who promised immortality? The Maker of the universe alone; the Great Artist and Father has formed us, such a living image as man is. But your Olympian Jove, the image of an image, greatly out of harmony with truth, is the senseless work of Attic hands. For the image of God is His Word, the genuine Son of Mind, the Divine Word, the archetypal light of light; and the image of the Word is the true man, the mind which is in man, who is therefore said to have been made "in the image and likeness of God," assimilated to the Divine Word in the affections of the soul, and therefore rational; but effigies sculptured in human form, the earthly image of that part of man which is visible and earth-born, are but a perishable impress of humanity, manifestly wide of the truth. That life, then, which is occupied with so much earnestness about matter, seems to me to be nothing else than full of insanity. And custom, which has made you taste bondage and unreasonable care, is fostered by vain opinion; and ignorance, which has proved to the human race the cause of unlawful rites and delusive shows, and also of deadly plagues and hateful images, has, by devising many shapes of demons, stamped on all that follow it the mark of long-continued death. Receive, then, the water of the word; wash, ye polluted ones; purify yourselves from custom, by sprinkling yourselves with the drops of truth. The pure must ascend to heaven. Thou art a man, if we look to that which is most common to thee and others—seek Him who created thee; thou art a son, if we look to that which is thy peculiar prerogative—acknowledge thy Father. But do you still continue in your sins, engrossed with pleasures? To whom shall the Lord say, "Yours is the kingdom of heaven?" Yours, whose choice is set on God, if you will; yours, if you will only believe, and comply with the brief terms of the announcement; which the Ninevites having obeyed, instead of the destruction they looked for, obtained a signal deliverance. How, then, may I ascend to heaven, is it said? The Lord is the way; a strait way, but leading from heaven, strait in truth, but leading back to heaven, strait, despised on earth; broad, adored in heaven.

Then, he that is uninstructed in the word, has ignorance as the excuse of his error; but as for him into whose ears instruction has been poured, and who deliberately maintains his incredulity in his soul, the wiser he appears to be, the more harm will his understanding do him; for he has his own sense as his accuser for not having chosen the best part. For man has been otherwise constituted by nature, so as to have fellowship with God. As, then, we do not compel the horse to plough, or the bull to hunt, but set each animal to that for which it is by nature fitted; so, placing our finger on what is man's peculiar and distinguishing characteristic above other creatures, we invite him—born, as he is, for the contemplation of heaven, and being, as he is, a truly heavenly plant—to the knowledge of God, counseling him to furnish himself with what is his sufficient provision for eternity, namely piety. Practice husbandry, we say, if you are a husbandman; but while you till your fields, know God. Sail the sea, you who are devoted to navigation, yet call the whilst on the heavenly Pilot. Has knowledge taken hold of you while engaged in military service? Listen to the commander, who orders what is right. As those, then, who have been overpowered with sleep and drunkenness, do ye awake; and using your eyes a little, consider what mean those stones which you worship, and the expenditure you frivolously lavish on matter. Your means and substance you squander on ignorance, even as you throw away your lives to death, having found no other end of your vain hope than this. Not only unable to pity yourselves, you are incapable even of yielding to the persuasions of those who commiserate you; enslaved as you are to evil custom, and, clinging to it voluntarily till your last breath, you are hurried to destruction: "because light is come into the world, and men have loved the darkness rather than the light," while they could sweep away those hindrances to salvation, pride, and wealth, and fear, repeating this poetic utterance: —

> "Whither do I bear these abundant riches? and whither
> Do I myself wander?"

If you wish, then, to cast aside these vain phantasies, and bid adieu to evil custom, say to vain opinion: —

"Lying dreams, farewell; you were then nothing."

For what, think you, O men, is the Hermes of Typho, and that of Andocides, and that of Amyetus? Is it not evident to all that they are stones, as is the veritable Hermes himself? As the Halo is not a god, and as the Iris is not a god, but are states of the atmosphere and of the clouds; and as, likewise, a day is not a god, nor a year, nor time, which is made up of these, so neither is sun nor moon, by which each of those mentioned above is determined. Who, then, in his right senses, can imagine Correction, and Punishment, and Justice, and Retribution to be gods? For neither the Furies, nor the Fates, nor Destiny are gods, since neither Government, nor Glory, nor Wealth are gods, which last [as Plutus] painters represent as blind. But if you deify Modesty, and Love, and Venus, let these be followed by Infamy, and Passion, and Beauty, and Intercourse. Therefore Sleep and Death cannot reasonably any more be regarded as twin deities, being merely changes which take place naturally in living creatures; no more will you with propriety call Fortune, or Destiny, or the Fates goddesses.

And if Strife and Battle be not gods, no more are Ares and Enyo. Still further, if the lightnings, and thunderbolts, and rains are not gods, how can fire and water be gods? How can shooting stars and comets, which are produced by atmospheric changes? He who calls Fortune a god, let him also so call Action. If, then, none of these, nor of the images formed by human hands, and destitute of feeling, is held to be a God, while a providence exercised about us is evidently the result of a divine power, it remains only to acknowledge this, that He alone who is truly God, only truly is and subsists. But those who are insensible to this are like men who have drunk mandrake or some other drug. May God grant that you may at length awake from this slumber, and know God; and that neither Gold, nor Stone, nor Tree, nor Action, nor Suffering, nor Disease, nor Fear, may appear in your eyes as a god. For there are, in sooth, "on the fruitful earth thrice ten thousand" demons, not immortal, nor indeed mortal; for they are not endowed with sensation, so as to render them capable of death, but only things of wood and stone, that hold despotic sway over men insulting and violating life through the force of custom. "The earth is the Lord's," it is said, "and the fullness thereof." Then why darest thou, while luxuriating in the bounties of the Lord, to ignore the Sovereign Ruler? "Leave my earth," the Lord will say to thee. "Touch not the water which I bestow. Partake not of the fruits of the earth produced by my husbandry." Give to God recompense for your sustenance; acknowledge thy Master. Thou art God's creature. What belongs to Him, how can it with justice be alienated? For that which is alienated, being deprived of the properties that belonged to it, is also deprived of truth. For, after the fashion of Niobe, or, to express myself more mystically, like the Hebrew woman called by the ancients Lot's wife, are ye not turned into a state of insensibility? This woman, we have heard, was turned into stone for her love of Sodom. And those who are godless, addicted to impiety, hard-hearted and foolish, are Sodomites. Believe that these utterances are addressed to you from God. For think not that stones, and stocks, and birds, and serpents are sacred things, and men are not; but, on the contrary, regard men as truly sacred, and take beasts and stones for what they are. For there are miserable wretches of human kind, who consider that God utters His voice by the raven and the jackdaw, but says nothing by man; and honor the raven as a messenger of God. But the man of God, who croaks not, nor chatters, but speaks rationally and instructs lovingly, alas, they persecute; and while he is inviting them to cultivate righteousness, they try inhumanly to slay him, neither welcoming the grace which comes from above, nor fearing the penalty. For they believe not God, nor understand His power, whose love to man is ineffable; and His hatred of evil is inconceivable. His anger augments punishment against sin; His love bestows blessings on repentance. It is the height of wretchedness to be deprived of the help which comes from God. Hence this blindness of eyes and dullness of hearing are more grievous than other inflictions of the evil one; for the one deprives them of heavenly vision, the other robs them of divine instruction. But ye, thus maimed as respects the truth, blind in mind, deaf in understanding, are not grieved, are not pained, have had no desire to see heaven and the Maker of heaven, nor, by fixing your choice on salvation, have sought to hear the Creator of the universe, and to learn of Him; for no hindrance stands in the way of him who is bent on the knowledge of God. Neither childlessness, nor poverty, nor obscurity, nor want, can hinder him who eagerly strives after the knowledge of God; nor does any one who has conquered by brass or iron the true wisdom for himself choose to exchange it, for it is vastly preferred to everything else. Christ is able to save in every place. For he that is fired with ardor and admiration for righteousness, being the lover of One who needs nothing, needs himself but little, having treasured up his bliss in nothing but himself and God, where is neither moth, robber, nor pirate, but the eternal Giver of good. With justice, then, have you been compared to those serpents who shut their ears against the charmers. For "their mind," says the Scripture, "is like the serpent, like the deaf adder, which stoppeth her ear, and will not hear the voice of the charmers." But allow yourselves to feel the influence of the charming strains of sanctity, and receive that mild word of ours, and reject the deadly poison, that it may be granted to you to divest yourselves as much as possible of destruction, as they have been divested of old age. Hear me, and do not stop your ears; do not block up the avenues of hearing, but lay to heart what is said. Excellent is the medicine of immortality! Stop at length your groveling reptile motions. "For the enemies of the Lord," says Scripture, "shall lick the dust." Raise your eyes from earth to the skies, look up to heaven, admire the sight, cease watching with outstretched head the heel of the righteous, and hindering the way of truth. Be wise and harmless. Perchance the Lord will endow you with the wing of simplicity (for He has resolved to give wings to those that are earth-born), that you may leave your holes and dwell in heaven. Only let us with our whole heart repent, that we may be able with our whole heart to contain God. "Trust in Him, all ye assembled people; pour out all your hearts before Him." He says to those that have newly abandoned wickedness, "He pities them, and fills them with righteousness." Believe Him who is man and God; believe, O man. Believe, O man, the living God, who suffered and is adored. Believe, ye slaves, Him who died; believe, all ye of human kind, Him who alone is God of all men. Believe, and receive salvation as your reward. Seek God, and your soul shall live. He who seeks God is busying himself about his own salvation. Hast thou found God? —then thou hast life. Let us then seek, in order that we may live. The reward of seeking is life with God. "Let all who seek Thee be glad and rejoice in Thee; and let them say continually, God be magnified." A noble hymn of God is an immortal man, established in righteousness, in whom the oracles of truth are engraved. For where but in a soul that is wise can you write truth? where love? where reverence? where meekness? Those who have had these divine characters impressed on them, ought, I think, to regard wisdom as a fair port whence to embark, to whatever lot in life they turn; and likewise to deem it the calm haven of salvation: wisdom, by which those who have betaken themselves to the Father, have proved good fathers to their children; and good parents to their sons, those who have known the Son; and good husbands to their wives, those who remember the Bridegroom; and good masters to their servants, those who have been redeemed from utter slavery. Oh, happier far the beasts than men involved in error! who live in ignorance as you, but do not counterfeit the truth. There are no tribes of flatterers among them. Fishes have no superstition: the birds worship not a single image; only they look with admiration on heaven, since, deprived as they are of reason, they are unable to know God. So are you not ashamed for living through so many periods of life in impiety, making yourselves more irrational than irrational creatures? You were boys, then striplings, then youths, then men, but never as yet were you good. If you have respect for old age, be wise, now that you have reached life's sunset; and albeit at the close of life, acquire the knowledge of God, that the end of life may to you prove the beginning of salvation. You have become old in superstition; as young, enter on the practice of piety. God regards you as innocent children. Let, then, the Athenian follow the laws of Solon, and the Argive those of Phoroneus, and the Spartan those of Lycurgus: but if thou enroll thyself as one of God's people, heaven is thy country, God thy lawgiver. And what are the laws? "Thou shalt not kill; thou shalt not commit adultery; thou shalt not seduce boys; thou shalt not steal; thou shalt not bear false witness; thou shalt love the Lord thy God." And the complements of these are those laws of reason and words of sanctity which are inscribed on men's hearts: "Thou shalt love thy neighbor as thyself; to him who strikes thee on the cheek, present also the other;" "thou shalt not lust, for by lust alone thou hast committed adultery." How much better, therefore, is it for men from the beginning not to wish to desire things forbidden, than to obtain their desires! But ye are not able to endure the austerity of salvation; but as we delight in sweet things, and prize them higher for the agreeableness of the pleasure they yield, while, on the other hand, those bitter things which are distasteful to the palate are curative and healing, and the harshness of medicines strengthens people of weak stomach, thus custom pleases and tickles; but custom pushes into the abyss, while truth conducts to heaven. Harsh it is at first, but a good nurse of youth; and it is at once the decorous place where the household maids and matrons dwell together, and the sage council-chamber. Nor is it difficult to approach, or impossible to attain, but is very near us in our very homes; as Moses, endowed with all wisdom, says, while referring to it, it has its abode in three departments of our constitution—in the hands, the mouth, and the heart: a meet emblem this of truth, which is embraced by these three things in all—will, action, speech. And be not afraid lest the multitude of pleasing objects which rise before you withdraw you from wisdom. You yourself will spontaneously surmount the frivolousness of custom, as boys when they have become men throw aside their toys. For with a celerity unsurpassable, and a benevolence to which we have ready access, the divine power, casting its radiance on the earth, hath filled the universe with the seed of salvation. For it was not without divine care that so great a work was accomplished in so brief a space by the Lord, who, though despised as to appearance, was in reality adored, the expiator of sin, the Savior, the clement, the Divine Word, He that is truly most manifest Deity, He that is made equal to the Lord of the universe; because He was His Son, and the Word was in God, not disbelieved in by all when He was first preached, nor altogether unknown when, assuming the character of man, and fashioning Himself in flesh, He enacted the drama of human salvation: for He was a true champion and a fellow-champion with the creature. And being communicated most speedily to men, having dawned from His Father's counsel quicker than the sun, with the most perfect ease He made God shine on us. Whence He was and what He was, He showed by what He taught and exhibited, manifesting Himself as the Herald of the Covenant, the Reconciler, our Savior, the Word, the Fount of life, the Giver of peace, diffused over the whole face of the earth; by whom, so to speak, the universe has already become an ocean of blessings.

CHAPTER XI. —HOW GREAT ARE THE BENEFITS CONFERRED ON MAN THROUGH THE ADVENT OF CHRIST.

Contemplate a little, if agreeable to you, the divine beneficence. The first man, when in Paradise, sported free, because he was the child of God; but when he succumbed to pleasure (for the serpent allegorically signifies pleasure crawling on its belly, earthly wickedness nourished for fuel to the flames), was as a child seduced by lusts, and grew old in disobedience; and by disobeying his Father, dishonored God. Such was the influence of pleasure. Man, that had been free by reason of simplicity, was found fettered to sins. The Lord then wished to release him from his bonds, and clothing Himself with flesh—O divine mystery! —vanquished the serpent, and enslaved the tyrant death; and, most marvelous of all, man that had been deceived by pleasure, and bound fast by corruption, had his hands unloosed, and was set free. O mystic wonder! The Lord was laid low, and man rose up; and he that fell from Paradise receives as the reward of obedience something greater [than Paradise]— namely, heaven itself. Wherefore, since the Word Himself has come to us from heaven, we need not, I reckon, go any more in search of human learning to Athens and the rest of Greece, and to Ionia. For if we have as our teacher Him that filled the universe with His holy energies in creation, salvation, beneficence, legislation, prophecy, teaching, we have the Teacher from whom all instruction comes; and the whole world, with Athens and Greece, has already become the domain of the Word. For you, who believed the poetical fable which designated Minos the Cretan as the bosom friend of Zeus, will not refuse to believe that we who have become the disciples of God have received the only true wisdom; and that which the chiefs of philosophy only guessed at, the disciples of Christ have both apprehended and proclaimed. And the one whole Christ is not divided: "There is neither barbarian, nor Jew, nor Greek, neither male nor female, but a new man," transformed by God's Holy Spirit. Further, the other counsels and precepts are unimportant, and respect particular things, —as, for example, if one may marry, take part in public affairs, beget children; but the only command that is universal, and over the whole course of existence, at all times and in all circumstances, tends to the highest end, viz., life, is piety, —all that is necessary, in order that we may live for ever, being that we live in accordance with it. Philosophy, however, as the ancients say, is "a long-lived exhortation, wooing the eternal love of wisdom;" while the commandment of the Lord is far-shining, "enlightening the eyes." Receive Christ, receive sight, receive thy light,

"In order that you may know well both God and man."

"Sweet is the Word that gives us light, precious above gold and gems; it is to be desired above honey and the honey-comb." For how can it be other than desirable, since it has filled with light the mind which had been buried in darkness, and given keenness to the "light-bringing eyes" of the soul? For just as, had the sun not been in existence, night would have brooded over the universe notwithstanding the other luminaries of heaven; so, had we nor known the Word, and been illuminated by Him; we should have been nowise different from fowls that are being fed, fattened in darkness, and nourished for death. Let us then admit the light, that we may admit God; let us admit the light, and become disciples to the Lord. This, too, He has been promised to the Father: "I will declare Thy name to my brethren; in the midst of the Church will I praise Thee." Praise and declare to me Thy Father God; Thy utterances save; Thy hymn teaches that hitherto I have wandered in error, seeking God. But since Thou leadest me to the light, O Lord, and I find God through Thee, and receive the Father from Thee, I become "Thy fellow-heir," since Thou "wert not ashamed of me as Thy brother." Let us put away, then, let us put away oblivion of the truth, viz., ignorance; and removing the darkness which obstructs, as dimness of sight, let us contemplate the only true God, first raising our voice in this hymn of praise: Hail, O light! For in us, buried in darkness, shut up in the shadow of death, light has shone forth from heaven, purer than the sun, sweeter than life here below. That light is eternal life; and whatever partakes of it lives. But night fears the light, and hiding itself in terror, gives place to the day of the Lord. Sleepless light is now over all, and the west has given credence to the east. For this was the end of the new creation. For "the Sun of Righteousness," who drives His chariot over all, pervades equally all humanity, like "His Father, who makes His sun to rise on all men," and distils on them the dew of the truth. He hath changed sunset into sunrise, and through the cross brought death to life; and having wrenched man from destruction, He hath raised him to the skies, transplanting mortality into immortality, and translating earth to heaven—He, the husbandman of God,

> "Pointing out the favorable signs and rousing the nations
> To good works, putting them in mind of the true sustenance;"

having bestowed on us the truly great, divine, and inalienable inheritance of the Father, deifying man by heavenly teaching, putting His laws into our minds, and writing them on our hearts. What laws does He inscribe? "That all shall know God, from small to great;" and, "I will be merciful to them," says God, "and will not remember their sins." Let us receive the laws of life, let us comply with God's expostulations; let us become acquainted with Him, that He may be gracious. And though God needs nothing let us render to Him the grateful recompense of a thankful heart and of piety, as a kind of house-rent for our dwelling here below.

> "Gold for brass,
> A hundred oxen's worth for that of nine;"

that is, for your little faith He gives you the earth of so great extent to till, water to drink and also to sail on, air to breathe, fire to do your work, a world to dwell in; and He has permitted you to conduct a colony from here to heaven: with these important works of His hand, and benefits in such numbers, He has rewarded your little faith. Then, those who have put faith in necromancers, receive from them amulets and charms, to ward off evil forsooth; and will you not allow the heavenly Word, the Savior, to be bound on to you as an amulet, and, by trusting in God's own charm, be delivered from passions which are the diseases of the mind, and rescued from sin? —for sin is eternal death. Surely utterly dull and blind, and, like moles, doing nothing but eat, you spend your lives in darkness, surrounded with corruption. But it is truth which cries, "The light shall shine forth from the darkness." Let the light then shine in the hidden part of man, that is, the heart; and let the beams of knowledge arise to reveal and irradiate the hidden inner man, the disciple of the Light, the familiar friend and fellow-heir of Christ; especially now that we have come to know the most precious and venerable name of the good Father, who to a pious and good child gives gentle counsels, and commands what is salutary for His child. He who obeys Him has the advantage in all things, follows God, obeys the Father, knows Him through wandering, loves God, loves his neighbor, fulfils the commandment, seeks the prize, claims the promise. But it has been God's fixed and constant purpose to save the flock of men: for this end the good God sent the good Shepherd. And the Word, having unfolded the truth, showed to men the height of salvation, that either repenting they might be saved, or refusing to obey, they might be judged. This is the proclamation of righteousness: to those that obey, glad tidings; to those that disobey, judgment. The loud trumpet, when sounded, collects the soldiers, and proclaims war. And shall not Christ, breathing a strain of peace to the ends of the earth, gather together His own soldiers, the soldiers of peace? Well, by His blood, and by the word, He has gathered the bloodless host of peace, and assigned to them the kingdom of heaven. The trumpet of Christ is His Gospel. He hath blown it, and we have heard. "Let us array ourselves in the amour of peace, putting on the breastplate of righteousness, and taking the shield of faith, and binding our brows with the helmet of salvation; and the sword of the Spirit, which is the word of God," let us sharpen. So the apostle in the spirit of peace commands. These are our invulnerable weapons: armed with these, let us face the evil one; "the fiery darts of the evil one" let us quench with the sword-points dipped in water, that, have been baptized by the Word, returning grateful thanks for the benefits we have received, and honoring God through the Divine Word. "For while thou art yet speaking," it is said, "He will say, Behold, I am beside thee." O this holy and blessed power, by which God has fellowship with men! Better far, then, is it to become at once the imitator and the servant of the best of all beings; for only by holy service will any one be able to imitate God, and to serve and worship Him only by imitating Him. The heavenly and truly divine love comes to men thus, when in the soul itself the spark of true goodness, kindled in the soul by the Divine Word, is able to burst forth into flame; and, what is of the highest importance, salvation runs parallel with sincere willingness—choice and life being, so to speak, yoked together. Wherefore this exhortation of the truth alone, like the most faithful of our friends, abides with us till our last breath, and is to the whole and perfect spirit of the soul the kind attendant on our ascent to heaven. What, then, is the exhortation I give you? I urge you to be saved. This Christ desires. In one word, He freely bestows life on you. And who is He? Briefly learn. The Word of truth, the Word of incorruption, that regenerates man by bringing him back to the truth—the goad that urges to salvation—He who expels destruction and pursues death—He who builds up the temple of God in men, that He may cause God to take up His abode in men. Cleanse the temple; and pleasures and amusements abandon to the winds and the fire, as a fading flower; but wisely cultivate the fruits of self-command, and present thyself to God as an offering of first-fruits, that there may be not the work alone, but also the grace of God; and both are requisite, that the friend of Christ may be rendered worthy of the kingdom, and be counted worthy of the kingdom.

CHAPTER XII. —EXHORTATION TO ABANDON THEIR OLD ERRORS AND LISTEN TO THE INSTRUCTIONS OF CHRIST.

Let us then avoid custom as we would a dangerous headland, or the threatening Charybdis, or the mythic sirens. It chokes man, turns him away from truth, leads him away from life: custom is a snare, a gulf, a pit, a mischievous winnowing fan.

> "Urge the ship beyond that smoke and billow."

Let us shun, fellow-mariners, let us shun this billow; it vomits forth fire: it is a wicked island, heaped with bones and corpses, and in it sings a fair courtesan, Pleasure, delighting with music for the common ear.

> "Hie thee hither, far-famed Ulysses, great glory of the Achæans; Moor the ship, that thou mayest hears diviner voice."

She praises thee, O mariner, and calls the illustrious; and the courtesan tries to win to herself the glory of the Greeks. Leave her to prey on the dead; a heavenly spirit comes to thy help: pass by Pleasure, she beguiles.

> "Let not a woman with flowing train cheat you of your senses, With her flattering prattle seeking your hurt."

Sail past the song; it works death. Exert your will only, and you have overcome ruin; bound to the wood of the cross, thou shalt be freed from destruction: the word of God will be thy pilot, and the Holy Spirit will bring thee to anchor in the haven of heaven. Then shalt thou see my God, and be initiated into the sacred mysteries, and come to the fruition of those things which are laid up in heaven reserved for me, which "ear hath not heard, nor have they entered into the heart of any."

> "And in sooth methinks I see two suns,
> And a double Thebes,"

said one frenzy-stricken in the worship of idols, intoxicated with mere ignorance. I would pity him in his frantic intoxication, and thus frantic I would invite him to the sobriety of salvation; for the Lord welcomes a sinner's repentance, and not his death.

Come, O madman, not leaning on the thyrsus, not crowned with ivy; throw away the mitre, throw away the fawn-skin; come to thy senses. I will show thee the Word, and the mysteries of the Word, expounding them after thine own fashion. This is the mountain beloved of God, not the subject of tragedies like Cithæron, but consecrated to dramas of the truth,—a mount of sobriety, shaded with forests of purity; and there revel on it not the Mænades, the sisters of Semele, who was struck by the thunderbolt, practicing in their initiatory rites unholy division of flesh, but the daughters of God, the fair lambs, who celebrate the holy rites of the Word, raising a sober choral dance. The righteous are the chorus; the music is a hymn of the King of the universe. The maidens strike the lyre, the angels praise, the prophets speak; the sound of music issues forth, they run and pursue the jubilant band; those that are called make haste, eagerly desiring to receive the Father.

Come thou also, O aged man, leaving Thebes, and casting away from thee both divination and Bacchic frenzy, allow thyself to be led to the truth. I give thee the staff [of the cross] on which to lean. Haste, Tiresias; believe, and thou wilt see. Christ, by whom the eyes of the blind recover sight, will shed on thee a light brighter than the sun; night will flee from thee, fire will fear, death will be gone; thou, old man, who saw not Thebes, shalt see the heavens. O truly sacred mysteries! O stainless light! My way is lighted with torches, and I survey the heavens and God; I become holy whilst I am initiated. The Lord is the hierophant, and seals while illuminating him who is initiated, and presents to the Father him who believes, to be kept safe for ever. Such are the reveries of my mysteries. If it is thy wish, be thou also initiated; and thou shall join the choir along with angels around the unbegotten and indestructible and the only true God, the Word of God, raising the hymn with us. This Jesus, who is eternal, the one great High Priest of the one God, and of His Father, prays for and exhorts men.

"Hear, ye myriad tribes, rather whoever among men are endowed with reason, both barbarians and Greeks. I call on the whole race of men, whose Creator I am, by the will of the Father. Come to Me, that you may be put in your due rank under the one God and the one Word of God; and do not only have the advantage of the irrational creatures in the possession of reason; for to you of all mortals I grant the enjoyment of immortality. For I want, I want to impart to you this grace, bestowing on you the perfect boon of immortality; and I confer on you both the Word and the knowledge of God, My complete self. This am I, this God wills, this is symphony, this the harmony of the Father, this is the Son, this is Christ, this the Word of God, the arm of the Lord, the power of the universe, the will of the Father; of which things there were images of old, but not all adequate. I desire to restore you according to the original model, that ye may become also like Me. I anoint you with the ungent of faith, by which you throw off corruption, and show you the naked form of righteousness by which you ascend to God. Come to Me, all ye that labor and are heavy laden, and I will give you rest. Take My yoke upon you, and learn of Me; for I am meek and lowly in heart: and ye shall find rest to your souls. For My yoke is easy, and My burden light."

Let us haste, let us run, my fellow-men—us, who are God-loving and God-like images of the Word. Let us haste, let us run, let us take His yoke, let us receive, to conduct us to immortality, the good charioteer of men. Let us love Christ. He led the colt with its parent; and having yoked the team of humanity to God, directs His chariot to immortality, hastening clearly to fulfill, by driving now into heaven, what He shadowed forth before by riding into Jerusalem. A spectacle most beautiful to the Father is the eternal Son crowned with victory. Let us aspire, then, after what is good; let us become God-loving men, and obtain the greatest of all things which are incapable of being harmed—God and life. Our helper is the Word; let us put confidence in Him; and never let us be visited with such a craving for silver and gold, and glory, as for the Word of truth Himself. For it will not, it will not be pleasing to God Himself if we value least those things which are worth most, and hold in the highest estimation the manifest enormities and the utter impiety of folly, and ignorance, and thoughtlessness, and idolatry. For not improperly the sons of the philosophers consider that the foolish are guilty of profanity and impiety in whatever they do; and describing ignorance itself as a species of madness, allege that the multitude are nothing but madmen. There is therefore no room to doubt, the Word will say, whether it is better to be sane or insane; but holding on to truth with our teeth, we must with all our might follow God, and in the exercise of wisdom regard all things to be, as they are, His; and besides, having learned that we are the most excellent of His possessions, let us commit ourselves to God, loving the Lord God, and regarding this as our business all our life long. And if what belongs to friends be reckoned common property, and man be the friend of God—for through the mediation of the Word has he been made the friend of God—then accordingly all things become man's, because all things are God's, and the common property of both the friends, God and man.

It is time, then, for us to say that the pious Christian alone is rich and wise, and of noble birth, and thus call and believe him to be God's image, and also His likeness, having become righteous and holy and wise by Jesus Christ, and so far already like God. Accordingly this grace is indicated by the prophet, when he says, "I said that ye are gods, and all sons of the Highest." For us, yea us, He has adopted, and wishes to be called the Father of us alone, not of the unbelieving. Such is then our position who are the attendants of Christ.

"As are men's wishes, so are their words;
As are their words, so are their deeds;

And as their works, such is their life."

Good is the whole life of those who have known Christ.

Enough, methinks, of words, though, impelled by love to man, I might have gone on to pour out what I had from God, that I might exhort to what is the greatest of blessings—salvation. For discourses concerning the life which has no end, are not readily brought to the end of their disclosures. To you still remains this conclusion, to choose which will profit you most—judgment or grace. For I do not think there is even room for doubt which of these is the better; nor is it allowable to compare life with destruction.